The
Black Toad

The
Black Toad

by
Gemma Gary

with foreword by Michael Howard

Line illustrations by the author
Photography by Jane Cox

TROY BOOKS

First North American Edition, 2020
First Printing, 2020
ISBN 978-0-7387-6569-3

Originally published by Troy Books Inc. 2012
ISBN 978-1-9561043-7-3

Llewellyn Publications is a registered trademark of Llewellyn Worldwide Ltd.

Cataloging-in-Publication Programme data is on file with the British National Bibliography.

Llewellyn Worldwide Ltd. does not participate in, endorse, or have any authority or responsibility concerning private business transactions between our authors and the public.

All mail addressed to the author is forwarded but the publisher cannot, unless specifically instructed by the author, give out an address or phone number.

Any Internet references contained in this work are current at publication time, but the publisher cannot guarantee that a specific location will continue to be maintained. Please refer to the publisher's website for links to authors' websites and other sources.

Llewellyn Publications
A Division of Llewellyn Worldwide Ltd. 2143 Wooddale Drive
Woodbury, MN 55125-2989 www.llewellyn.com

Printed in the United States of America

Acknowledgements

With grateful thanks to;
Jane Cox, Christine Gary, Michael Howard, Graham King
and Hannah Fox of the Museum of Witchcraft, John
Caple, Nigel G. Pearson, Kelvin Jones, JackDaw and the
work of Cecil Williamson.

Contents

Line Illustrations and Figures
By Author

Photographs

By Jane Cox

Foreword

By Michael Howard

ISTORICALLY the West Country has always been a land of mystery, myth and magic. Gemma Gary's new book The Black Toad explores the magical aspect of south-west England and its reputation for witchcraft. It deals especially with Devon and Cornwall, which until the coming in of the Great Western Railway in the 1830s was a fairly remote area cut off from the rest of the country. In such conditions superstition and a popular belief in charms, curses and the power of the witch, survived long after it had been banished by the forces of rationalism elsewhere.

Even in the distant past a belief in witchcraft, sorcery and the power of the old pagan gods survived in the West Country for several hundred years after other parts of Britain had been converted to the new religion. Christianity was introduced into the region during the fourth and fifth centuries CE, originally in its Roman and Celticised forms.. However some parts of Cornwall remained pagan until at least the end of the fifth-century and perhaps even after.

With the intrusion of the Saxons and the Danes into Somerset, Dorset and Devon some previously Christianised rural areas temporarily reverted back to the Old Faith and the worship of the Old Gods as they did in Kent and East Anglia.

In the sixth century there was an influx of missionaries from Wales and Brittany into the West Country, and many are now remembered today as 'Celtic saints'. One of these was an abbot and bishop called Sampson or Samson (480-560 CE). He was the son of a royal princess and a Welsh chieftain who had fostered the princes of the ancient kingdoms of Gwent and Dyfed. During his missionary work among the 'pagan savages' of Cornwall, Samson met an elderly woman who had eight sisters (making up the mystical and magical lunar number of nine). He discovered that they were all dedicated followers of the Old Ways. Samson challenged the old crone to abandon her wicked and false beliefs and embrace the 'true religion'. When she refused it is said that the saint used the power of God to strike her dead. His battle with an old witch-woman with grey shaggy hair, wearing red garments and holding a trident or three-pronged stave has been interpreted as either an encounter with a representation of a Celtic goddess or one of her priestesses.

In another story about Samson's visit to Cornwall, it was said he found the ignorant natives dancing on a hilltop around a heathen idol. This was in the hope of encouraging a good harvest. Because it was around Lammastide or Lughnasadh, at the beginning of August, it is possible the image was one of the Celtic god Lugh or his British equivalent. The saint demanded that the pagans stop their blasphemous rite, but they merely laughed and ignored him. Then a young boy rode up and when his horse stumbled in a rabbit hole he was thrown heavily to the ground. There he lay as if dead. Samson saw his chance to impress the distraught natives and achieve his aim. He persuaded them to agree to stop their 'devil-worship' if, by a miracle, he could bring the boy back to life. As the fallen rider was probably only unconscious this would not have been a difficult task. When the saint revived the boy the pagans were so amazed and impressed at his magical powers they immediately converted to Christianity. Samson also had a nearby prehistoric standing stone used in pagan rituals transformed into a Celtic Christian cross.

Although it is not suggested that there is any direct historical and physical continuity between the pre-Christian pagan and magical beliefs of the ancient past and the practices of the early modern witches and cunning folk described by Gemma Gary, the folk memory of the Old Ways can still be detected in what they believed in and did. It also survives in the magical praxis of modern followers and practitioners of the Elder Faith and the Craft. Those few who adhere to the traditional ways of witchcraft that are sometimes called 'the true persuasion'.

As described in Gemma's book, these traditional ways include the patronage and guardianship of ancient sacred sites used for seasonal rites and magical workings, a belief in the genii loci (the wights or spirits of the land) and the realm of Faerie and the Otherworld, the utilising of elemental forces such as storms, thunder and lightning for magic and the mystical significance of the natural world and its fauna and flora. The latter includes the recognition of the spiritual power of totemic animals and birds and 'green magic' or wortcunning - the esoteric knowledge and lore of healing and protective herbs, natural poisons and psychoactive plants and fungi such as mandrake and the fly agaric toadstool.

The transition between the old paganism and early Christianity is also reflected in the dual faith observance of West Country witches and cunning folk. This is graphically illustrated by the charms that Gemma provides in her book. These include invocations to Jesus, the magical use of psalms for blessing and cursing, and the binding of charms and spells by the holy trinity of the Father, Son and Holy Ghost. The employment of such Christian religious formulae was regarded as quite normal by practitioners of the Arte Magical and the Old Craft in the past. Today it has only survived in more traditional witch circles in the West Country and elsewhere.

In the deep wooded valleys, on the wild desolate moors and the wave lashed seashores of the south-west of England the witch and the wizard, the cunning man and the wise-woman, the charmer and the peller still practise their bright and dark arts. Ordinary people leave out offerings to the Good People, the piskies and the pixies, while claiming that the bowls of milk and honey are "for the hedgehogs". The Wild Hunt with its demon hounds roams Exmoor and Dartmoor on dark and stormy nights harvesting the souls of the dead. Across the West Country when the moon is full covens gather to work the Old Magic. As their ancestors did before them, they revere the Horned One or Man in Black by his traditional names of Bucca Dhu, Dewar, Old Nick and the Devil, and honour his consort the dark and bright Queen of Elfhame.

For all those who are interested in learning about the Old Path as it is taught and practised today by West Country witches, this book of practical magic and sorcery will be a revelation. As the late Cecil Williamson, founder of the witchcraft museum in Boscastle, North Cornwall and a modern cunning man himself, said and Gemma Gary's excellent book proves – "It still goes on today."

Michael Howard
Beltane 2012

"Clutching my father's hand, we knocked at the door of an old thatch-roofed apology for a house, entered in response to a thin, reedy voice piping "Come in," and stumbled our way across a nearly dark room, lit only by a tiny window, a foot square and mostly stuffed with rags. All sorts of dried herbs and mysterious things were hanging from the rafters overhead, but – most mysterious of all – away by an open fireplace, sitting on a stool, smoking a small pipe, was old Rose herself, looking in the shadows to be my childish ideal of a witch. What especially appealed to me was her claw-like hands…"

Memory of "Old Rose" related to Hamilton-Jenkin by Mrs Stanley James.

Introduction

IT was an experience once so common to the ordinary folk of the West Country, to make their way to consult a Wise practitioner of repute when in need or distress. Their journey may have taken them some considerable distance and time, on foot or by drawn cart, at a time when few 'roads' were extant, and those that were would hardly be considered worthy of being named as such today. Others, more fortunate, would have in their more convenient locality such a practitioner, dwelling quite possibly at the edge of their village or community, set apart, marked out and 'different' from the people, yet ever watchful and observant of them.

Walking tentatively down the long thorny path to the cottage door, there might the client be called in to find the wise-woman, cunning-man, charmer, 'white witch' or fairy-doctor, sitting in their window, silently gazing out into a reality revealed only to their sight. They may already know why their visitor has come, and simply send them away to find their problem resolved without a word leaving the client's lips. Others may search for the cause and solution within their hearth fire, the rising smoke, or a soot blackened glass.

Yet others may disappear into another room, or partitioned off area, there to consult with the spirits, after some time to emerge with charms, substances or instructions to be followed by their client faithfully.

We are repeatedly educated, by the detached and distant academic historian, that such ways have long died out in their entirety here in the West Country. At best they will receive just a polite smile and a nod from those who are still compelled to seek assistance from magical practitioners, and indeed from the practitioners themselves who still serve those who consult them to seek advice from the oracular artes, for counsel, for rites of healing and exorcism, for charms and substances to lift ill-influences or draw to them that which is desired or needed. That both client and practitioner still exist in the West Country, as surely they must do elsewhere, is fact undeniable. It is also unforgivably lazy, and ignorant in the extreme, to readily dismiss those drawn to the practice in the contemporary day as unauthentic, simply for the crime of existing in a time when they may be subject to many and varied modern developments and trends within the occult and witchcraft revival. The traditionalist practitioner is discerning and pragmatic, making use of all that works. Indeed, if Mr. G. B. Gardner's Craft was available to nineteenth century practitioners, is it really so inconceivable that they would employ from it those things that they found to be of use and discard the rest?

The traditional Craft is, by its very nature, operative and results orientated, and it is in its successes and its ability to serve that its authenticity resides, and is the very reason for its continued presence. The seeking of assistance and the inclination to learn the ways to give that assistance still survive and evolve in the present day, and will continue to do so a lot longer yet.

For the contemporary practitioner, here are provided ways and means that have been employed here in the West Country, both in previous centuries and in more recent times.

The ways here explored may be quite unfamiliar, or even uncomfortable, to some practitioners of modern Craft, from whom any notion that cursing and magical retribution may be a possibility of their path has been thoroughly trained out. However, the traditional practitioner accepts all the artes of the spirits and the Old Ones, but in the hopes they may never have cause to use all of them. Even some of those newly come to the contemporary traditional Craft, particularly those across the Atlantic Ocean, in my experience are likely to look awkwardly upon the ceremonial and grimoire derived practices in their eagerness to distance themselves from the ceremony of their cousins the Wica, and hold a perhaps understandable desire to form a Craft that is entirely rustic and intuitive in its simplicity. The fact cannot be ignored though, that our historical forebears embraced the grimoire tradition as soon as it became available to them, and the ceremonial actions, words and designs that were found to be of use became an intrinsic part of our native folk magical tradition, where magical signs, planetary hours, working circles and the virtues of the directions have long since been employed. Both are likely also to be ill at ease regarding the presence of Christian magic, but it is an established part of the tradition, and all that is of use is employed, even if the grimoire it is drawn from is named The Holy Bible. Despite a belief in, and working relationship with, the spirit world, otherworldly forces and the old pacts with 'The Old One', folk-magical practitioners are traditionally dual-observers and have long professed a faith in Christianity, though not necessarily in its Church, and have employed its magic alongside that of their Old

Ways and Fairy Faith. Faith is all important in the success of magical operations, and the client is more often than not going to be of the Christian faith. For them, a charm that calls upon the aid of God the Father, God the Son, and God the Holy Ghost, is naturally going to be strengthened by their faith, and thus more likely to succeed.

One consideration, that may or may not be unique to Cornwall and the West Country, is the matter of discerning between the witch and the cunning person. It would appear, in most parts of the British Isles, to be the case that a clear line exists between the Witches, and the Cunning Folk. The former is entirely malevolent in nature, devoting their arte to causing disaster and suffering to man and beast, whilst the latter exists to counter the evil of the former, to lift their influence from their victims, in addition to providing general cures, divinations, counsel, and other beneficent services. Things are literally not quite so 'black and white' when considering the Cornish and West Country practitioner. Here the two roles merged, and the name "witch" seems to have been largely interchangeable with those of wise-woman, cunning-man, charmer and pellar, sometimes with the highly misleading prefix of "white". Here, the local folk-magical practitioner was just as likely to bring down curses upon those who in some way offended them, as they were to provide clients with cures and to lift the ill-influence of other aggrieved practitioners.

The old and deep-rooted beliefs in witchcraft, magic, and the dreaded and much feared influence of the black witch's eye, lingered on much longer here in the West Country, particularly in Cornwall. This remote South-Westerly horn of land was at one time home to many witches and practitioners of the folk-ceremonial magic artes, in particular its most remote region; West Penwith. Here both historical accounts and fantastic folk-tales of the activities of witches abound. The presence of such practitioners, both 'white' and 'black', and the popular beliefs surrounding them, reached a great intensity in the late nineteenth century. This was still a time when Cornwall was very remote, 'other from' and little connected with the rapidly 'advancing' and modernising England. It was thus in this 'Otherworldly' landscape of haunted hills, ancient stone temples of our pre-Christian ancestors, and potent Holy Wells of healing and divinatory virtue, that a people, naturally given to mystical and superstitious temperament, held steadfastly to their traditional witch-beliefs.

Power and Preparation

✠

IN the beginning of workings and rites of the Way, there are a number of considerations and measures, via which they may be undertaken with greater potency.

Times Wisht and Hood

First the practitioner must consider the timing of the work. The virtues of the heavenly fires, the work that they aid, their days and hours, are of great concern in timing. Of vital importance to the West Country practitioner is the phase of the moon, and its cycle of increase and decrease, in all their operations, and its virtues are called upon further by the employment of the numbers three and nine within all ritual actions, and repetitions of muttered incantation and prayer.

The times betwixt, when the division between the worlds of man and spirit loses what little solidity it may have, are in the West Country the 'wisht' or 'hood' times; moments bewitched or empowered. Charms, workings, rites, and all operations of the Way, undertaken at these times will be greater in potency; for greater aid from the spirits and the spirit forces may be called upon by the practitioner. Such times are of course the times of dusk, dawn, midnight, and the eave of the 'High Nights'.

Loci Wisht and Hood

Following timing, the locus of the work may be considered. Wisht and hood places are loci of the spirits and the way between the worlds, and so, at such places, may the spirits' aid and the spirit-forces be made available in greater abundance to the practitioner who calls upon them.

Within the West Country, much lore exists around the lonely and wind distorted Whitethorn, a tree taboo, under which children were warned from resting for fear that they will be taken away by the spirits into their world. Under the Whitethorn is a place wisht and hood, and where the practitioner, in genuflection, may call upon the potent aid of the spirits to aid their operations.

The meandering serpentine streams are visually potent boundaries and are thus places betwixt. By the nature of their flowing water, they are also places of highly useful kinetic spirit-force, of great use within many operations of the Way. Within all such operations, where the taking up of waters from the stream is called for, it is vital that the following method is observed. The pitcher or vessel used must, with great care, be simultaneously lowered into the water and moved with the stream's flow, matching also its speed, in order that its flow be not disturbed or interrupted. Via this carefully observed action, the potent spirit-force of the stream will be captured within the water removed from it. The very same is observed in the taking of such things as pebbles or stones from the bed of the stream, to be later employed within some working.

The home hearth of the practitioner is their very own betwixt place, wisht and hood, where workings may be potently performed; for it is the loci of the fire at the very heart of the home and, by its very nature, a portal where much power may be drawn upon. Via the hearth and chimney may the spirit-force and will be sent forth to perform the work desired, but it is also the prime means of entry into the home for forces and influences that are unwelcome and, as such, it is a place to be potently protected. The hearth of the 'black witch' traditionally also becomes of concern in lifting the influence of their ill wish and evil eye.

Light from the dark; Sundry Impedimenta & Aids to Power
Of aid to the raising of power, drawing upon spirit-force, and calling to the practitioner the assistance of spirit helpers, are a number of items and ways known in the West Country. Items that may be sought after and carefully collected by the practitioner to attract and enhance working power and spirit-force include such ordinary things as seeds, nuts and eggs. Such are potently symbolic vessels and containers of life and spirit-force, thus also emblematic of productivity, fecundity, creation itself; the emergence of new life, power, and magic. They are protective also; bearing the outer shell guarding that which grows within, thus, via such charms may the practitioner hope to guard her operations and endeavours from failure. Thus we see why shells, nuts, seeds and eggs of all kinds may find their way to being incorporated into the very fabric of the West Country practitioner's charms and working impedimenta.

The shells of snails are favoured also, not only for their protective shell, but for their traditional associations in the West Country with power – sexual force, fertility, fecundity and creation. Also here are the creatures credited with the ability to bestow blessings upon places and people, thus are their shells gathered to fashion charms to bring protection, potency, passion and good fortune upon the home and life endeavours of their keeper.

Serpents and horses are emblematic also of power and magical force. The bones of both creatures are coveted, along with the hair of horses, to be carried, or installed within the home along with the impedimenta of the working horse, as fetishes and charms of power and magical potency.

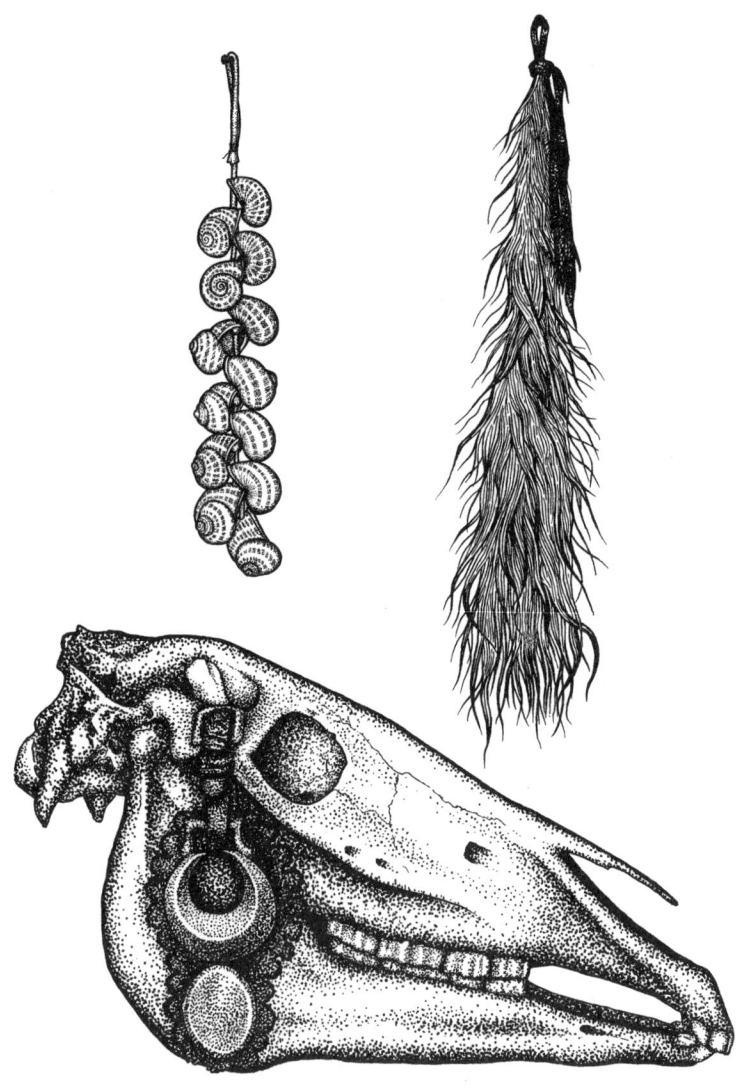

Beans are associated in West Country tradition with the spirits of the dead, and are kept and carried with other substances of cognate association; such as thyme, elder and elm, and with written charms. Such a charm bestows upon the practitioner the ability to have at their bidding the powers, blessings and wisdom of the shades of the dead.

Wands and staves are the 'roads of power' via which magical force and virtue may be stirred, drawn upon or sent forth by the practitioner. The shaft of the traditional broom is likewise a road of spirit-force, and the whole device is itself a steed of power. The broom is emblematic also of the sexual union, being the phallic shaft thrust deep into the feminine brush, thus of the creative powers so vital to the working of magic and the warding of evil. This steed of power is thus 'ridden' by the practitioner within their circle of arte, sometimes with the provision of a candle or lantern affixed to the end of the shaft. The practice brings to the magic making of the practitioner the creative, generative and fertile forces, adding to its potency and bringing the endeavour to fruit.

Yet more efficacy may be brought to the operation by jumping through fire upon the ridden broom. The fire, the smoke that rises from it and the wind that carries it forth, are all highly useful tools to the West Country practitioner. The fire at the midst of the practitioner's circle of arte, is the light of creation from the void. The magical will of the practitioner is born forth, by the creative magical act, carried aloft within the rising smoke, by the aid of the spirits will it manifest, or be carried forth to exert its influence upon the target of the work. In the latter case, the direction of the wind is of high importance.

From the ceremonial artes has entered into the Craft of the West Country practitioner, the Pentacle of Arte. Upon these devices are inscribed such things as the Pentagram; the four

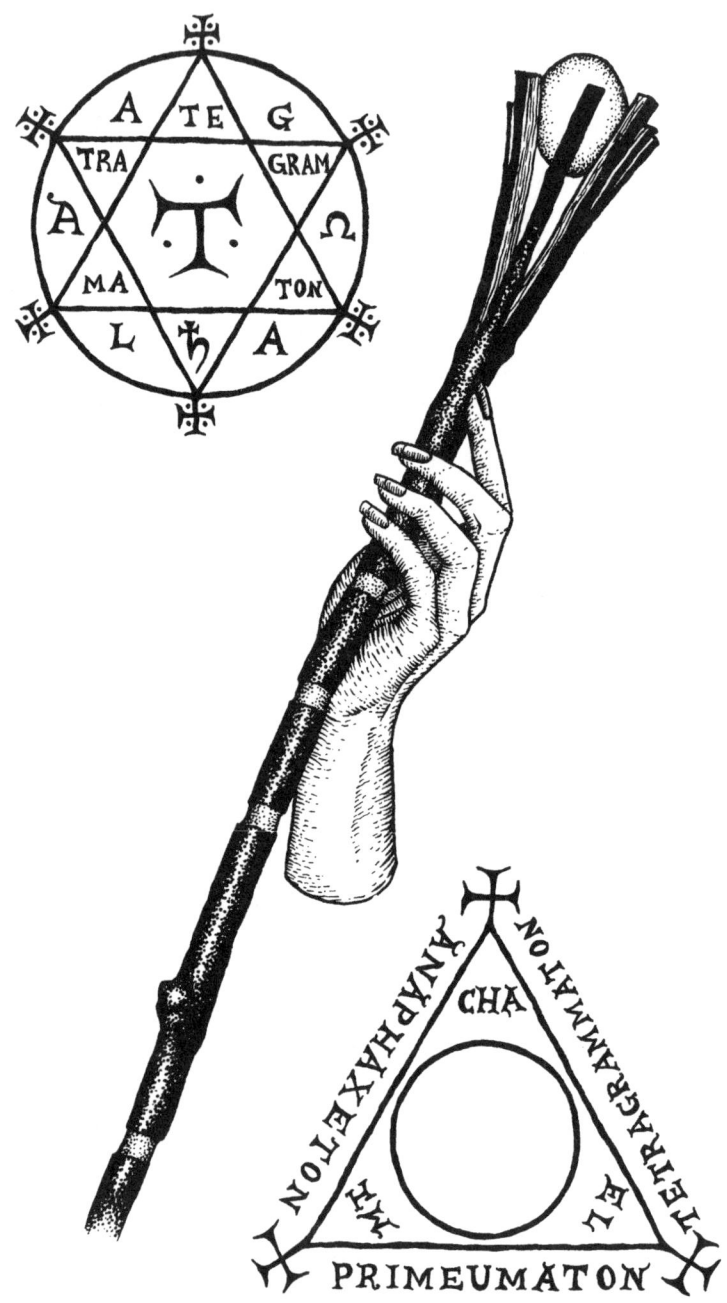

elements of the manifest world beneath quintessence; 'All in One', the source and the animating spirit. The design is contained within the circle of the infinite.

The emblem of the pentagram may be reduced into the simple form of the cross; the four elements of each arm conjoined at their midst in quintessence.

The design is simplified further, in other examples, in the encircled triangle; the triplicity of creation, the quintessential source; 'All in One', above the opposing forces of manifest nature.

For the practitioner, the pentacle of arte is a tool emblematic of creation itself, and the causal elements of the material world, from which that which is magically desired may be brought forth into manifestation in accordance with the will.

Upon such a device may charms and substances of the arte be placed in order that the pertinent force may be manifest into their form, and the desire for which they were created to bring into being may be brought forth into manifestation. Fires and thuribles of smouldering substances are also placed upon the pentacle of arte in order that the desires for which they burn may issue forth into manifest reality.

Charms, fetishes, and other items created and empowered to manifest magical desire, are kept in West Country practice within the 'charm box'. Some examples are crafted to be in the form of a coffin, for that which is placed within it is intended to bring about the death of a situation so that a new set of circumstances may be born forth. Thus the physical relics of the working are held within while the working takes effect.

It is thus cognate with the 'wish box' and those containers used to be magically rid of things undesired. What is placed within is left for the spirits to see to, until that which is desired has been brought about.

Beginning Rites and Workings

At the place chosen for the undertaking of the work, the practitioner will first ensure that everything required for the rite is prepared and in its proper place. With arms upraised, and holding the working staff, in the dextral or sinistral hand depending on the working being one of conjuration or exorcism, the practitioner will declaim;

"Ecce benedicite Domino omnes servi Domini qui statis in domo Domini,
In noctibus levate manus vestras ad sanctum et benedicite Domino,
Benedicat tibi Dominus ex Sion factor caeli et terrae"

Then shall a circle be marked out, around the place of working, upon the ground with the staff. The direction of this marking, and the hand in which the staff is held being sinistral or dextral, will again be determined by the nature of the rite.

Then shall be called unto the place the spirits and virtues that shall aid the work. The operation of calling may be aided greatly by various methods which, in traditional thought, are held to draw the aid of the spirits to the West Country practitioner. It is held that fumigations are of use not only in exorcism, and sending forth the will, but in drawing to the practitioner the aid of spirits, when they are pleasing in scent. In addition to sweet smelling substances cast upon the flames of a working fire, or upon the coals of a thurible, the West Country practitioner may employ a simple spirit calling device in the form of a switch of twigs, such as the woody parts of the sage, bound at one end. The other end lit from the flames of the working fire will smoulder and issue forth sweet smelling smoke as the practitioner runs around the place, waving the device as they go. The fumes will not only exorcise ill and impeding influences from the place, but draw the attention of those helpful spirits. Sound is also of use within such an operation. The 'wind roarer' is of use in the calling of spirits, the raising of useful forces and in encouraging a powerful shift in consciousness and atmosphere. By swinging the device to rotate within the air, and by adjusting its speed, can sounds of a bizarre, throbbing and unearthly nature be created. Having heard a number of times multiple 'wind roares' in use at meetings of the Wise, and once caught the eerie cry of one in use by some solitary practitioner, carrying across the still and misty air of the far western Cornish landscape, I can attest to the potency of these devices. Drumming, and the winding of instruments of horn and bone have their traditional use for these purposes also. Whatever devices are employed, or none, the practitioner will make their call;

> *"I summon and conjure thee powers of the ways above and below,*
> *I summon and conjure thee to arise, come ye hither and appear;*
> *Red spirits of fire, white spirits of earth, grey spirits of water,*
> *and black spirits of air!*
> *In the Old Master's name I summon and conjure thee spirits and*
> *powers of the six ways; Arise! Come ye hither, appear, and aid*
> *me in my work!"*

The practitioner will then be ready to enter into their work. Once the work is complete, it is meet to splash some mouthfuls of some good drink, and perhaps scatter some food about the working place, in thanks to the spirits that have come to the practitioner's aid.

Old Mother Red-Cap

✠

Witch-Fire - Power, Protections & Desire

LREADY have certain materials and items been described; gathered and kept generally about the practitioner and their abode to aid and bring increase to their gathering of power, potency and spirit force. Some are fashioned into charms, others incorporated into tools and working items of the arte.

One particular charm to bring increase unto the powers and healing abilities of the practitioner is a 'Wise-woman's Magical Bag' from the Honiton District.

Its outer form is to be made from blood red silk. Into this are bound various items of virtue; such as plant materials in the form of wildflower seeds of many varieties, dried herbs of potency and curative virtue, and the scrapings of dried roots. Animal materials are included also; the feathers of birds for the virtue of air via which spirits and spirit forces may easily travel and be conveyed. The feet of the quick, cunning and stealth rats and mice; and those of the dark, slow and earthly hidden moles are included also. Most potent is the inclusion of the feet of toads; those most mysterious creatures, dwelling betwixt the waters and the earth, who are most intimately bound with the ways of the witch. Added to this charm are the hair and nail parings of the practitioner to be blessed with increased power and the healing spirit-force. The whole is together bound shut within the red silk, blessed and kept ever close by or upon the person of the practitioner.

Another charm bag for power, to bring increased potency to the practitioner's powers and skills in witchcraft and the divinatory artes, is formed from the Yarrow, or 'Devil's Rattle'. The practitioner must visit and search the graveyards, until a grave is found upon which is growing the Yarrow. At midnight must the witch return to the churchyard and visit the grave in order to harvest the herb, to be bound and kept within a black cloth. This charm will be made all the more potent if the grave from which the herb is gathered is that of a man died young.

The famed loadstone is another of the virtuous materials of nature, gathered by the practitioner, kept to draw and gather unto them powers of use to their craft. Also are the lodestones supplied to the practitioner's clients, enclosed within the charm bags of their trade, to add to their potency and to draw unto the client that which is desired. It is offered to clients as a stone of great power and spirit-force, protection and drawing one's desires.

The Cornish witch might also greatly covet the Piskies' Grinding-stones, or Mill-stones; the enchanting name given unto the ancient spindle whorls that may be brought from the earth into the light of day by action of the farmer's plough. Both their romantic association with the Faery Folk (which may not be all that romantic when one considers that for many a West Country witch, the Piskey are the spirits of the ancestors), the symbolically magical action of the mill-stone, and their actual association with the abundant magical lore surrounding the work of spinning and threads make it easy to see why such an item might be prized as an amulet of power and spirit-force.

In old West Country belief, the rolling of great storms and thunder over the land is traditionally attributed to the power of the Old One; a power the witch is ever keen to imbibe of. Thus, during such occasions in Cornish tradition, whilst many might shutter themselves in to await the return of calm and safety, the wise will instead throw open their doors and windows to invite the great potency of the Old One, as the lightening flashes and the thunder claps and rumbles about the skies, into their homes and into their work. It is a power also associated with good fortune; scarcely a thing to be cowered from.

Numerous are the ways and tools via which the witch's gathered and accumulated powers may be sent forth to convey their will and magical intent. A particularly effectual exemplar from the West Country, utilising a good number of traditionally potent and virtuous components, is that practice that has come to be known as the 'witch's ladder', or the 'wishing rope'. The West Country practitioner will have a length of good cord, or rope; not at all too great in thickness. Into this must be tied the feathers of crow and of goose, alternately and at regular intervals. To the bottom of this is tied the holed hag-stone, wishing-stone, or whispering-stone, and at the top of the rope is tied a loop. The wishing rope is either held in the hand, or hung upon a nail in a beam; by either method, a vessel of coals upon which is set to burn substances of pertinent virtue is prepared and set directly beneath the wishing rope. The witch will then set the rope swinging to and fro through the rising smoke as they mutter their spell of influence, be it for good or for ill. Throughout the entire operation, the mind and will of the practitioner must be firmly affixed upon the intent of the working, and from the very beginning of the wishing rope's construction.

Concurrent within this practice is the employment of cord or thread magic; the spirit road or track of power along the length of which required virtues and potencies can be drawn to one, or one's will and influence sent forth. It is also the strand of fate; either of one's own fate, or that of a client or other target of the working, altered, re-formed and influenced by the tying of knots of will and desire. The feathers tied along its length are cognate with the virtues of air and of the winds, via which spirits, virtues and the witch's influence may travel and be conveyed to one or sent forth. The holed hag-stone, so often co-employed with cord or thread magic, is for the folk-magician a 'faery portal' through which requests can be made to the spirits and Otherworldly powers, for magical desires and needs to be born forth into manifestation in this world. The swinging motion of the wishing rope is of great aid to the trance-like and meditational working focus of the witch; for all repetitive and rhythmic actions take the mind to that place betwixt so useful to the working of magic. The smoke of the burning herbs is likewise of aid to the achievement of this useful state, but assists greatly also in the attracting of useful spirits and the raising of power. As the wishing rope swings to and fro through the rising smoke as it issues forth, so the prayers, will and influence of the witch are up-born to do their work.

In West Country belief we find that the spittle of the witch is a vehicle of their will and power, and thus their magical influence. The very act of spitting within the traditional practices of the country witch is to impart their will imbued power and influence, which may be enacted by numerous modus operandi. In workings upon an individual, either for good or for ill, the witch might extravasate her 'venom' upon the doorstep of the intended target, or upon some article intimate to them, with accompanying mutterings of blessing or malediction. Within acts of healing the practitioner may impart the healing influence by ejecting upon the client's ailing body part, or a representation of it, spittle or a mouthful of stream water gathered by ceremony for the use. Spittle may also be forcefully cast into the working fire, again with accompanying magical utterances of intent that the witch's will may manifest or be sent forth to do its work. Likewise is the 'witch's breath' a potent conveyer and vehicular vessel of power and virtue. Both the accumulated power and spirit-force, to which the body of the witch has by arte been made host, and those potencies, virtues and spirits conjured within the rites and magical work of the practitioner, may in pure focus of will and intent be imparted and issue forth upon such things as places, charms, parts of the body and magical likenesses skilfully crafted by the witch's hand. By this arte may charms be empowered to their work, places charged with influence and the healing or baneful influences alike be imparted upon the body of the recipient or their likeness.

Protections and Defences

✠

Stone Cross and Witch-Bottle

The ancient stone markers of the ways, hewn with the cross of the worlds, stand silently for the protection and sanctity of place, and, to the wise, they offer aid in the defence against the black witch's curse and ill-wish. The equal armed cruciform wheel unites the ways above, below, and the midguard landscape, also the cardinal ways of the four directions, and the spiritual world - vertical axis, and the material world - horizontal axis, encircled as one. Thus the stone cross draws upon the virtues of all worlds, and extends a warding influence to all ways. As a symbol of the meeting of 'all in one', or the centre of all, the cross also depicts the divine force.

The Village of St Buryan, from where I write, has such crosses erected at the ends of each of the five roads that extend out from the village's centre. Perhaps, then, a village well protected, it is certainly a village with a long history of old magic, from where the influences of its magical practitioners continue to be sent forth, in all directions, to work upon their targets.

To these stone crosses, the old Cornish might come to kneel and petition the ways, and the divine, for protection, exorcism and release from ill fortune, curses and all evil influences.

The 70th Psalm – to be recited for deliverance from the evil of one's enemies;

'Make haste, O God, to deliver me; make haste to help me, O Lord.
Let them be ashamed and confounded that seek after my soul: let them be turned backward, and put to confusion, that desire my hurt.
Let them be turned back for a reward of their shame that say, Aha, aha.

Let all those that seek thee rejoice and be glad in thee: and let such as love thy salvation say continually, let God be magnified.
But I am poor and needy: make haste unto me, O God: thou art my help and my deliverer; O Lord, make no tarrying.'

It has also been the practice in Cornwall to make burials at the foot of at least one stone cross of 'witch-bottles'; a favourite prescription of the cunning practitioner, and 'white witch', for the lifting and countering of curses suffered by their clients at the hands of the 'black' practitioner.

The methods for creating this device are many, yet vary in only minor details. The following method derives from early 18th Century Cornish instruction;

To make a defence against ill-wishers, heat one's own urine until it is scalding and pour this into a narrow necked stone jug. As much salt as can be taken up between two fingers and the thumb of the left hand must be added. Take then three new nails, sharpen the ends to the sharpest points and put these into the jug, points downwards. Close the jug firmly with clay and bind tightly with leather. It must immediately then be placed into warm embers and not allowed once to go cold for nine nights. The ill-wisher will be greatly tormented by this and will have no power over you.

Such devices of counter-magic, work via the ancient principle that there exists a link between 'witch' and 'bewitched'. The urine, being of the body of the victim, will thus contain part of the 'vital essence of the witch' within it. Contained within the urine will be traces of the victim's blood, and, it is suggested by old witch-belief, there is to be found some of the witch's own blood also; *for such is the subtlety of the Devil, that he will not suffer the witch to infuse any poisonous matter into the body of man or beast, without some of the witches blood mingled with it'.*

Blagrove, 1671.

Such a notion is cognate with the ancient belief that a witch's blood is the vessel and vehicle of their power, and that if their blood were to be drawn forth from 'above the breath' by their victim, then the spell will be broken and their power is lost.

By this link between the witch and the victim, and the inclusion of the victim's urine, and other matter from their body within the witch-bottle, is opened a conduit via which magical retaliation becomes possible. By the heat of the embers is the witch tormented, particularly in the passing of water, by the sharpened nails is the witch pricked and stabbed at. Three in number, they may recall the nails of the crucifixion, but also the three areas the witch seeks to influence via their magic – the mind, the body, and the soul, and the causing of madness, bodily ailment or injury, and spiritual attack; causing general misfortune and haunting by evil spirits. The three nails may also be seen to represent the three ways in which a witch may operate – via form, force, and spirit. The physical world equips the Witch with herbs, stones, and other substances and materials to employ, known to the witch are the ways to conjure, raise and direct the forces of land, the waters, the winds and the heavenly fires, and they are proficient in the summoning of spirits, conversing with them for wisdom and divinations, and sending them forth to carry out their will. Thus, in the three nails of the witch-bottle, we may have the arsenal of the witches, turned and redirected upon them. Also within our example we have salt – the traditional breaker of spells and a potent substance of exorcism. In the old stoneware vessels we have this substance present within the very salt-glaze coating them; bringing an increase to their efficacy.

Bottles for counter attack may, in Cornish tradition, also be buried. The bottled urine of the victim, man or beast, is to be buried neck downward, again inflicting upon the witch great difficulty with their water; causing them to suffer the torment of strangury. Buried witch-bottles might also cause the witch to suffer a slow and painful wasting death.

Other bottles may be prescribed that are pre-emptive and protective in nature, rather than charms of counter-attack. Again, such devices vary in detail with regard to their contents, although to a greater extent than those of counter-attack. Some may provide a 'decoy' representing the potential victim of a black witch's maleficia, or the attention of evil spirits. As such, they must of course contain something of the body of the person, or persons, they are to provide with protection. Hair and nail clippings are quite traditional. It is these items that will provide the decoy, attracting the attention of any curses or evil spirits, instead of their actual intended victim. Once drawn into the device, many tangled threads entrap and confuse the spirits or the curse, for such things are only happy to travel in straight lines. The inclusion of thorns, pins, or nails, again ensures that the trapped evil spirits, or the originator of any curses, is further ensnared, stabbed and pricked at. Salt, and other substances prepared, or prescribed, by the cunning practitioner, my provide exorcism and further protections.

Other protective bottles in Cornwall have contained earth and ash. Boundary earth taken from the four cardinal points of the area to be protected and the sanctified earth of a churchyard could be advised. The eternal ash of protective woods, herbs, or the written charms of the cunning practitioner would all provide potent protections.

Bottle charms of the pre-emptive protective kind are best housed beneath the hearth, within the chimney, or beneath the threshold, for these are of course the vulnerable portals of the home, where such things as curses and evil spirits may seek entry. As such, these are the advised locations for the installment of all household charms and devices of a protective nature.

Inscribed Charms for Protection

Here follow three written charms for the protection of the individual, to be worn or kept close to their person. Such written charms are to be presented folded and contained with a square bag of velvet or felt, or else contained, held and bound only by a cross of thread.

For a written charm to ensure that no foe need be feared; mark this design and writing;

Whosoever beareth this sign
Need fear no foe. So shall it be!

For those who are suffering from the ill-wish of the black witch, mark this square so that they may be healed and guarded from further intrusions of bewitchment;

A written charm to guard against fever, ague, or black witchcraft may be made by inscribing the following;

Whosoever does keep about their person this charm shall be never afflicted with fever, ague, or witchcraft;

When Jesus saw the cross, there to be crucified, Pilate said unto him "what aileth thee? Why shakest thou? Hast thou fever, ague or witchcraft" Jesus said unto him "I have neither fever, ague nor witchcraft, but shake for thy sins."

Fire Rites for Protection

Yet another traditional rite for the same is the old act of passing through fire. It is an ancient and powerful rite for the lifting, removal and exorcism of evil influences from people and from cattle, having them jump or pass thrice through the flames with the sun. It is also an act to encourage good fortune, strength, power, fecundancy and potency. The operation is more potently enacted upon Midsummer's Eve.

Upon this high night, circle-dances are traditionally performed around fires in Cornwall and the West Country. One at a time, the dancers break away from the ring to jump through the flames before circling madder and faster with linked hands; the dancers pull the ring to and fro through the fire until, by this action of treading, the flames are extinguished. By this rite it is believed the participants are guarded from the influences of evil and ill-fortune for a year.

To impart protections and blessings, and for the exorcism of evil bewitchments upon buildings and areas of land, a rite may be performed with fire. Burning torches are, at night, to be carried aloft at speed around the place nine times in the direction of the sun.

Protective Charm Bags and Amulets

A Cornish charm, from the town of Penzance, is here described to be created for the client who seeks a potent protection against all evil forces and ill-influences. This charm is crafted by the making of a bag of red flannel into which is placed a pinch of the protective and exorcising salt within a twist of red paper, and plant materials in the form of seven fiery pepper corns within a twist of blue paper, and a pinch of wood ash from the strong and solar oak within a twist of white paper. Two rose buds are included; one of red and one of white, before the addition of animal parts. The foot of a rabbit and the spur of a cock complete the contents which are together bound and sealed within their red flannel housing to be charmed and charged by the witch for their client.

A charm of cure and protection for those already in suffering from the ill-wishing of the black witch may be supplied in the form of a leathern bag. Within this is held the strange living metal, full of spirit-force; 'quick-silver' or mercury; there enclosed to be worn about the neck of the client.

Other charms against the evil influences and the black witch's eye include the magical maiden nail – of the fiery, earthy, red and bloody martial iron. Such may be kept within the pocket, or worn enclosed within a charm bag at the chest as an amulet against all ill-influence.

For more general protection, The Lord's Prayer may be supplied, written upon parchment and kept concealed within the boot as a charm against all calamity and misfortune. Likewise may coal form a fortunate charm against a variety of undesirable things. Most potent is coal discovered beneath the root of the Mugwort, or Plantain on that most potent night for magical protection; the eve of midsummer. This may be enclosed and kept to be worn as a charm against such maladies and dire misfortunes as plague, carbuncle, lightening, the quartan ague and burning.

Further Protective Rites and Measures

In all rites and operations against the black witch's curse and the lifting of ill-influence the practitioner may employ salt; this to be cast about the place, person or other to receive the exorcism and protection of the working. Likewise within such operations, and in the making of charms against evil bewitching both the practitioner and the client may employ the aid of the 68th Psalm;

"Let God arise, let his enemies be scattered: let them also that hate him flee before him.

As smoke is driven away, so drive them away: as wax melteth before the fire, so let the wicked perish at the presence of God.

But let the righteous be glad; let them rejoice before God: yea, let them exceedingly rejoice.

Sing unto God, sing praises to his name: extol him that rideth upon the heavens by his name JAH, and rejoice before him.

A father of the fatherless, and a judge of the widows, is God in his holy habitation.

God setteth the solitary in families: he bringeth out those which are bound with chains: but the rebellious dwell in a dry land.

O God, when thou wentest forth before thy people, when thou didst march through the wilderness; Selah:

The earth shook, the heavens also dropped at the presence of God: even Sinai itself was moved at the presence of God, the God of Israel.

Thou, O God, didst send a plentiful rain, whereby thou didst confirm thine inheritance, when it was weary.

Thy congregation hath dwelt therein: thou, O God, hast prepared of thy goodness for the poor.

The Lord gave the word: great was the company of those that published it.

Kings of armies did flee apace: and she that tarried at home divided the spoil.

Though ye have lien among the pots, yet shall ye be as the wings of a dove covered with silver, and her feathers with yellow gold.

When the Almighty scattered kings in it, it was white as snow in Salmon.

The hill of God is as the hill of Bashan; an high hill as the hill of Bashan.

Why leap ye, ye high hills? this is the hill which God desireth to dwell in; yea, the LORD will dwell in it for ever.

The chariots of God are twenty thousand, even thousands of angels: the Lord is among them, as in Sinai, in the holy place.

Thou hast ascended on high, thou hast led captivity captive: thou hast received gifts for men; yea, for the rebellious also, that the LORD God might dwell among them.

Blessed be the Lord, who daily loadeth us with benefits, even the God of our salvation. Selah.

He that is our God is the God of salvation; and unto GOD the Lord belong the issues from death.

But God shall wound the head of his enemies, and the hairy scalp of such an one as goeth on still in his trespasses.

The Lord said, I will bring again from Bashan, I will bring my people again from the depths of the sea:

That thy foot may be dipped in the blood of thine enemies, and the tongue of thy dogs in the same.

They have seen thy goings, O God; even the goings of my God, my King, in the sanctuary.

The singers went before, the players on instruments followed after; among them were the damsels playing with timbrels.

Bless ye God in the congregations, even the Lord, from the fountain of Israel.

There is little Benjamin with their ruler, the princes of Judah and their council, the princes of Zebulun, and the princes of Naphtali.

Thy God hath commanded thy strength: strengthen, O God, that which thou hast wrought for us.

Because of thy temple at Jerusalem shall kings bring presents unto thee.

Rebuke the company of spearmen, the multitude of the bulls, with

the calves of the people, till every one submit himself with pieces of silver: scatter thou the people that delight in war.
Princes shall come out of Egypt; Ethiopia shall soon stretch out her hands unto God.
Sing unto God, ye kingdoms of the earth; O sing praises unto the Lord; Selah:
To him that rideth upon the heavens of heavens, which were of old; lo, he doth send out his voice, and that a mighty voice.
Ascribe ye strength unto God: his excellency is over Israel, and his strength is in the clouds.
O God, thou art terrible out of thy holy places: the God of Israel is he that giveth strength and power unto his people. Blessed be God."

An old and wise practice, found within the West Country and beyond, to guard the home from the entry of the black witch's influence is to cross upon the hearth the iron fire-tools. A simple charm; potent in its form, its material and its location.

For the same need may a piece of bacon be selected and stuck with many pins. This device is then to be hung high within the chimney. Here we may ponder that the evil influence seeking entry into the home via the chimney will encounter this flesh before any other. Thus the bacon may be seen to act as a decoy, and the pins to prick and stab at the originator of the curse.

Another similar and powerful charm for the protection of the home, and its inhabitants and contents from the attentions and influences of evil spirits and ill-wishers is the stuck heart. The hearts of horses, or other large animals, stuck with many and countless thorns and pins may be secreted within the chimney, or within the roof space by being hung upon a beam, and there to be left undisturbed by the occupants in order that its protective influence may remain.

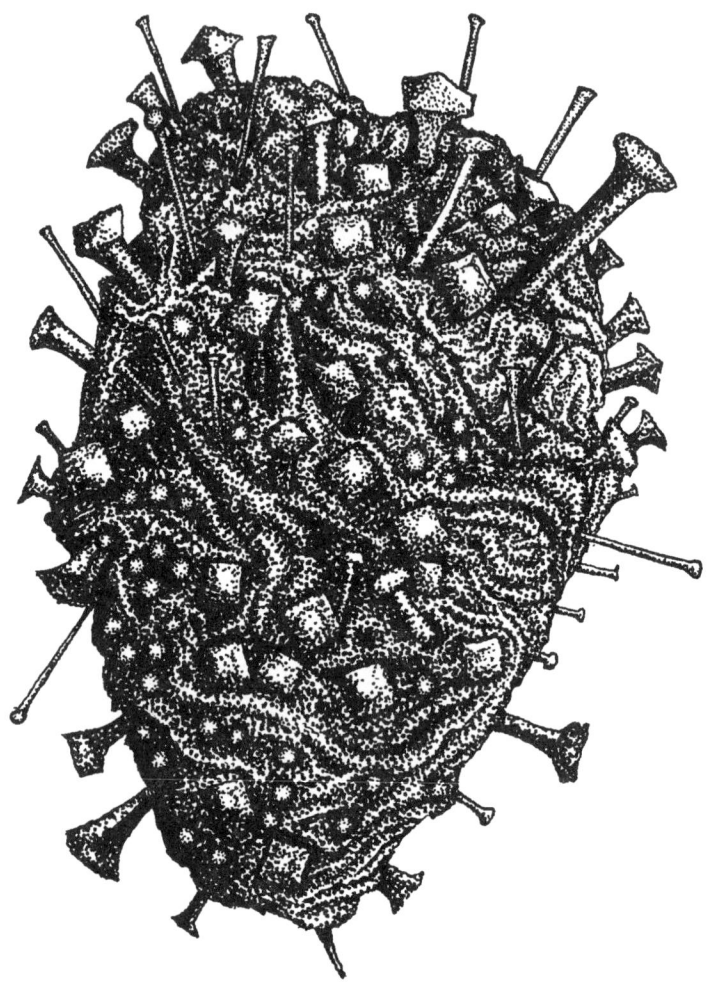

As well as the Hearth, the doorways into the home are also to be guarded with protective influences. Such signs as the pentagram may be cut into the sill of the door, and horseshoes traditionally fixed to the door itself and to the lintel above it. Such measures ensure that all evil spirits and influences are denied entry into the home.

A good general protective charm for the household, but in particular to bring upon the place protection from fires, is to have the slough of an adder hung, and there to stay, upon a roof-beam of the building.

Protections may be provided against hauntings by hanging up within the place where the apparition makes its appearances the skull of a horse. This, one would imagine, would have the added benefit of also providing a deterrent from the attention of intruders of a more corporeal nature. The lucky holed stone, or 'hag-stone', provides a more compact charm against spirits when hung within the bedroom.

The silvered backing of mirrors is, it is believed, thought to attract lightening, thus during a storm are all mirrors in the household covered to prevent lightening damage to the property.

There are protections also for the livestock of the household, numerously in the form of plant-charms as we shall see within the ways of the green artes. A charm specifically for the protection of animals who have gone missing appears in the simple act of hanging a pair of iron shears upon the main cross beam of the household. The charm brings assurance that the animal will come to no harm whilst missing from its home.

A Protective Charm against Drowning

A potent charm, highly sought-after and prized by fishermen, was formed from the child's birth caul or birth-cap. The keeping of this charm would ensure that those under its protective influence would never drown. Within some examples of the child's caul charm, are enclosed two inscribed parchment charms; the one being a true Mezuzah parchment, and upon the other is marked with *Ps. Cvii 29 In Te Domine Speravi.*

𝕮𝖚𝖗𝖊-𝕮𝖍𝖆𝖗𝖒𝖘 𝖆𝖓𝖉 𝕻𝖗𝖔𝖙𝖊𝖈𝖙𝖎𝖔𝖓𝖘 𝕬𝖌𝖆𝖎𝖓𝖘𝖙 𝕬𝖎𝖑𝖒𝖊𝖓𝖙
✠

Charming by Animal Parts

Various animals and their parts are to be found within the cure-charms of the West Country witch. Particularly potent within West Country tradition is the toad. Tradition informs us that there are two kinds of 'toad' being 'wet toads' and 'dry toads'. The former, being what we today would call frogs rather than toads, were believed to be of no great use to the practices of curative charming. The proper 'dry toad' is by tradition possessed of great curative virtue, and most potent of all are those known as 'sage bush toads', referring to those specimens found beneath the sage of the garden. Generally greatly beloved of the West Country witch as a creature of great beauty, mystery and power, in their demise their body and its parts may be employed within the ways of curative charming in the following ways.

For a charm against fever, the body of a toad must be dried thoroughly, and then pounded and ground into a powder. Enclose this within a bag to be worn beneath the armpit of those requiring the cure.

A toad blood-stopping charm may be crafted by having the body of a large toad, and three bricks. Within an oven, or a fire, the three bricks must be heated to a great intensity. Remove one of the bricks to the ground, and place the body of the toad upon it, there leaving it until the brick is cold.

The toad is removed and the brick is replaced to be heated before the next brick is brought out and the toad placed upon it. Again, when the brick has grown cold, the action is repeated with the last brick, and then again and again until the toad may be reduced to ashes. Carefully gathered, these ashes are to be enclosed within a silken bag one and a half inches square in size. When there is one who is bleeding, place the charm upon their heart and the bleed shall be made to stop.

An old charm for the bite of an adder employed the skin of a toad. This was to be placed upon the bite, and by virtue of the toad's immunity from the adder, so a cure was to be imparted.

For skin diseases, a toad cure-charm was created from the poison found in a toad's head. This was to be collected and enclosed within a leathern bag in size one inch square. This in turn was to be sewn into a bag of white silk with a neck-cord long enough so that it may be worn by the patient with the charm bag resting against the pit of their stomach. On the third day of wearing it the patient would be sick, the charm was then to be removed and buried. As the charm would rot, so would the patient be relieved of their condition.

A curative toad charm for 'The King's Evil' and sores in any limb could be made by having the corresponding body part of a toad. This was to be enclosed within a small charm bag and given to be worn by the patient.

Other Animal-Part Charms

For those suffering with cramp, the ankle bone of a hare may be given to be carried as a pocket charm.

The asthmatic condition could be charmed against by the patient wearing against their chest the skin of a mole.

Two animals and a suckling woman are required within one charm for shingles. For a male sufferer, together in a saucer is to be mixed blood collected from the tail or the ear of a she-cat, and from the comb or wattles of a hen. To these bloods must be added milk squeezed from the breast of a woman suckling a female child. The same procedure is to be followed for a female patient, but a tom cat, a cock, and a woman suckling a male child are to be used instead. In both cases, the resulting mixture is to be struck over the afflicted area and then dressed with "raw head".

Blood Stopping

The stopping of bleeds in both humans and animals has long been a prominent part of the practice of the traditional charmer, particularly in farming communities where accidents are an unfortunate commonality. As such there are a good number of charms for this purpose. Given the urgency of the situation, blood stopping was, and is, often performed by the charmer as an act of distant magic, or 'sending forth the spirit' if traveling to attend to the patient in physicality were to take too long. The practitioner may demand to know such things as who and where the patient is, where upon the body the wound is located, and how or by whom it was caused.

By one West Country method, the charmer will press their thumb to the part of their own body that corresponds to the location of the wound upon the patient's body. They will the begin to utter as they charm;

> *"And when I passed by thee (give name of the wounded) and saw thee polluted in thine own blood, I said unto thee, when thou wast in thy blood, Live; yea, I said unto thee when thou wast in thy blood, Live. Then washed I thee with water; yea, I thoroughly washed away thy blood from thee, and I anointed thee with oil. In the name of the Father and of the Son, and of the Holy Ghost. Amen! Amen! Amen!"*

If it is possible to attend to the patient in person, the charmer may work by making passes over the wound with their left hand against the sun. Whilst doing so they will utter in a way that is not clearly audible to their patient, nor to those around;

> *"Jesus was born in Bethlehem,*
> *Baptised in the river Jordon,*
> *When the water was wild in the wood,*
> *The person was just and good,*
> *God spake and the river stood,*
> *And so shall now thy blood,*
> *In the name of the Father, the Son, and the Holy Ghost.*
> *Amen, Amen, Amen."*

Another example:

> *"Christ our Lord was born in Bethlehem.*
> *He was baptized in the river of Jordan.*
> *The waters ran rude.*

He bid it to stand and it stood.
So shall the Blood of (patient's name) be still,
In the name of the Father and the Son and Holy Ghost.
Amen."

Say then thrice:

"Praise God may all things pass away."

There are methods also for stopping bleeding from the nose specifically. A charm bag may be made in red, in sympathy, and this being filled with pieces of red silk. The sealed charm bag is given to the patient to be worn about their neck. In another method, the only material requirement is a length of red ribbon. This is to be tied about the neck or the wrist of the patient. The sympathetic symbolism is overt and luculent; the red ribbon being the flow of the patient's bleed, and the knot tied within it is the desired flow stopping clot. More occult is the ribbon/cord as a means of drawing upon and sending power forth; the connection between practitioner and the imparting of influence and change to the patient's predicament by the knotting of their cord of fate.

As the spoken charms employed within the arte of blood-stopping invoke the stopping of the flowing holy waters, it is not surprising that tradition forbids the practitioner from crossing open flowing water on their return from treating a patient. Crossing all rivers, streams and the like is to be avoided, no matter how great the detour; for if such waters are crossed, the influence of the work will be lifted and the patient would begin to bleed again.

A Cure-Charm for the Thrush

The child must be brought, along with a long thread, down to a 'willis' or spring. There, holding the child in her arms under the spring, she must hold its tongue down with her finger. She must then cast the thread upstream so that it will flow towards her and the child. The thread is captured in its motion and drawn through the mouth of the child and around its head thrice whilst saying the eighth Psalm over it;

"O LORD, our Lord, how excellent is thy name in all the earth! who hast set thy glory above the heavens. Out of the mouth of babes and sucklings hast thou ordained strength because of thine enemies, that thou mightest still the enemy and the avenger. When I consider thy heavens, the work of thy fingers, the moon and the stars, which thou hast ordained; what is man, that thou art mindful of him? and the son of man, that thou visitest him? For thou hast made him a little lower than the angels, and hast crowned him with glory and honour. Thou madest him to have dominion over the works of thy hands; thou hast put all things under his feet: all sheep and oxen, yea, and the beasts of the field; the fowl of the air, and the fish of the sea, and whatsoever passeth through the paths of the seas. O LORD our Lord, how excellent is thy name in all the earth!"

Upon the third morning following this operation, the thread is brought again to the place where it is to be cast into the stream and there allowed to float away and out of sight so that the thrush will be taken away with it. This charm-rite will be all the more potent if the stream employed is one flowing eastward.

An alternative version of this cure involved the threading of six lengths of cotton through the open mouth of a compliant cat (if such exists), a procedure to be repeated, using the same threads, with the patient. These threads are then to be taken to a river and cast therein.

A simple rite employing flowing water may be performed to bring a cure for soreness in the throat. The one afflicted has only to pass over a stream three times.

For a Thorn in the Flesh

To extract a thorn from flesh, the practitioner may take the sloughed skin of an adder. This is to be applied and then drawn off the opposite part of the body to that which is afflicted.

The practitioner will utter over the wound as they perform thorn extraction charms;

"Our saviour Christ was prick with thorns, never rankled never fustered, no more shant thine (name) Out of the bone, into the fleash, out of the fleash into the skin, out of the skin into the Earth, in the name of the Father etc. Amen."

or

"Happy man that Christ was born!
He was crowned with a thorn:
He was pierced through the skin,
For to let the poison in;
But His five wounds, so they say,
Closed before He passed away.
In with healing, out with thorn:
Happy man that Christ was born!"

Old Mother Red-Cap

A Cure-Charm for Soreness in the Breasts

The charmer must obtain lead that has been stolen from a church, and form it into the shape of a heart, pierced so that it may be threaded upon a neck-cord and given to be worn by the patient.

For a Sprain

The practitioner shall utter over the injury as they charm;

> *"Our Lord Jesus Christ rode over a bridge. His horse lighted and He lighted. He said, "Marrow to marrow, and bone to bone, and sinews to sinews, and skin to skin (and to the others). In the name of the Father and the Son and of the Holy Ghost I cast this sprain away. Amen. So be it."*

For a Sleeping Limb

A limb that has 'fallen asleep' can be charmed back into life by anointing it thrice with one's spittle with the form of the cross.

The Healing Cage Charm

For injuries to limbs, the back, and where bones have been broken, a charm can be fashioned in the form of a healing cage. A bundle of thin, yet sturdy, sticks are bound at either end, and pulled lightly apart from each other at the middle so that within may be packed tightly a multitude of herbs and substances of healing and strengthening virtue. Through and around these taut bars of the cage, red ribbon is woven tightly to bind in the healing virtue of the serpent as the practitioner mutters words of encouragement to the operation.

For a Stye

The washing-pot stick is taken up to be passed through a wedding ring of gold. The charmer will hold then the ring in one hand to 'strike' with the other the afflicted eye whilst saying over it;

"pot-ee, pot-ee,
why dist pote me?
To pote the wan out of thine 'ee."

Pocket Charms Against Toothache and Rheumatism

As a certain cure and preventative against these maladies, one is advised, by the wisdom of old country folk, to carry in the pocket a potato, a lump of sulphur, or a lump of brimstone. For toothache specifically; the sufferer may pull, with their own teeth, a tooth from a disinterred human skull. This tooth is then to be carried in the pocket as a curative charm.

The Touch of the Dead to Cure the Living

There is a long history within West Country magical tradition of the cures that may be imparted by the dead, and by things connected to the dead, upon the living.

News of a man's death might in the past have brought visitors from miles around in hope of receiving the touch of the dead man's hand to cure diverse afflictions and maladies. The hand of the dead would be touched to the afflicted area, and passed downwards and leftwards, either three or nine times. The ritualistic touch of the dead was held to have the power to bring the death of the patient's affliction.

It was also believed that to touch the dead body would prevent one from dreaming of it, or from seeing it again. I can attest to the truth of this tradition, and that, conversely, the dead body of a loved one I had neither touched nor even seen had repeatedly haunted my dreams, whilst the dead that I have touched have visited only as they were in life.

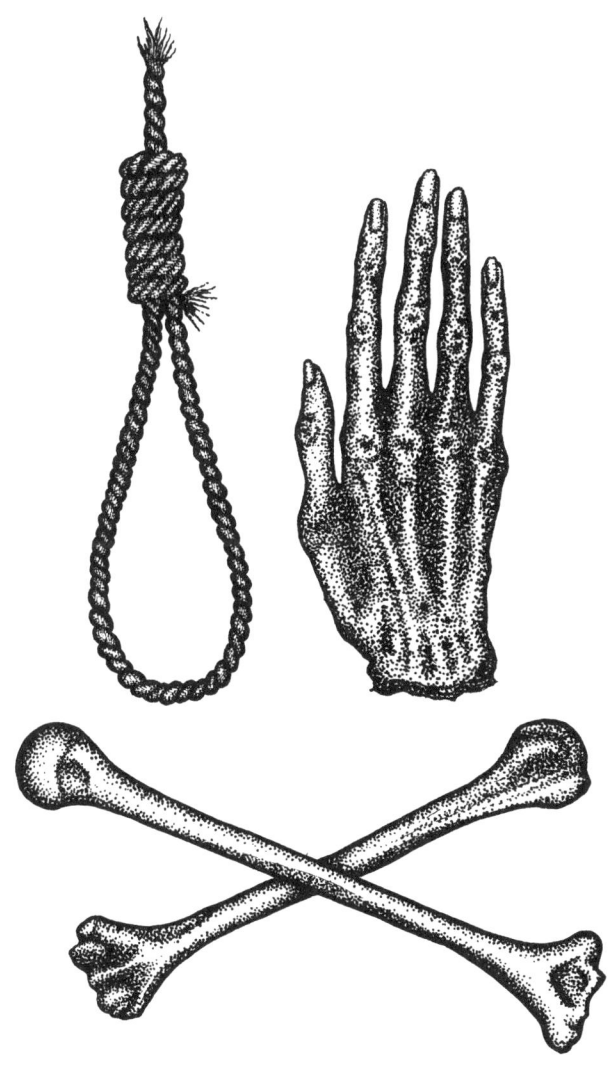

Relics of the dead are also, by tradition, possessed of curative virtue. As an old cure for fever a bone is kept, wrapped in cloth, from the body of a man, who in life had never suffered from the fever. The fever bone would be brought to the patient so that it may be put to lie for a while upon the chest of patient to bring upon them a cure.

The rope by which a man had died from hanging was a highly prized object of potent curative virtue. Such would be kept to be brought out by the charmer to impart cures by being touched to ailments to charm them away. The sought after rope would, for example, be placed around the head and then removed to cure headache. For the same malady would a snuff be made from moss that had grown upon the skull of a dead man.

A ring made from the handle of a coffin would be employed as a charm to be worn against cramp.

Sundry Methods of Wart Charming

Such are the myriad of wart charming methods employed within the West Country; often with each practitioner having their own modus operandi, to list them all would, if it were possible, provide enough material for at least a modest book devoted to the subject alone. Some methods, as we shall see later, belong to the craft of the 'Green Doctor' for their employment of plants, and as with the arte of blood-stopping, the wart charmer need not necessarily work in the physical presence of their client, but at a distance. In such cases there may not even be any discernable external, or revealed, modus operandi, and the charmer's requirement may be as simple as knowing how many warts their patient is in possession of.

Here follow a selection of wart charming methods of note employed within the West Country, as I dare say they are elsewhere also.

Wart Charming by 'Passing on Magic' - A stream must be sought whose water flows in a southwardly direction. From it are to be collected with care, being mindful not to interrupt the water's flow, white quartz stones. One stone is required for each wart possessed by the patient to which each stone will be touched three times. The stones are immediately to be enclosed within a bag, and this 'bag of warts' is to be taken to a crossroads at midnight; there to be discarded. Whosoever is driven by curiosity to pick up and open the bag shall have the warts, and the patient shall be relieved of the affliction. An alternative method for disposing of the 'bag of warts' is to hitch the bag loosely to the horn of a cow, leaving her to dispose of it where she will, to be found by some unfortunate who will become the next keeper of the warts.

Wart Burying - Cord magic may be employed by the practitioner having a length of parcel string. Along its length is to be tied one knot for each wart possessed by the patient; each of these knots being touched by the charmer to the wart they represent. This 'string of warts' is to be taken at midnight to the crossroads, there to be buried so that as the knots rot so will the warts go.

Flesh may also be employed to cure flesh; a piece of bacon; which must be stolen; is used to 'strike' the wart. This, again is to be taken to the crossroads at midnight, and there buried to rot in order to relieve the patient of their wart.

A particularly interesting burying charm involves cutting a piece of turf; one for each wart, and turning them to be replaced up-side-down. A rite of reversal and the turning of circumstance upon its head – what was green, now shall fade and so shall thy warts.

'Get-rid-of' magic, for that is essentially what wart charming is, may also call upon the aid of the dead to take with them the patient's affliction. To each wart is touched a pin; each of these being placed within a bottle. This charm-bottle is then to be taken to the graveyard; there to be buried within a new grave. As the pins turn to rust, so shall the warts fade and be gone.

Wart Charming by Fire - To be rid of warts by this method, the patient is to be taken to the home of the charmer and there brought to their hearth.

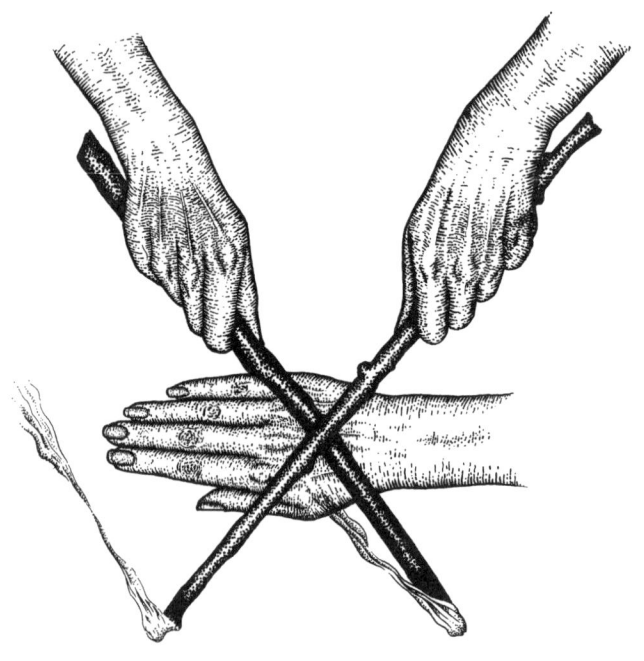

The author collecting water from a slow south-flowing stream.
Great care is taken to disrupt the flow as little as possible in order to
capture the useful spirit-force

Items of power and spirit-force used by the traditional West Country witch. From the author's colletion (above) and the Museum of Witchcraft, Boscastle (below)

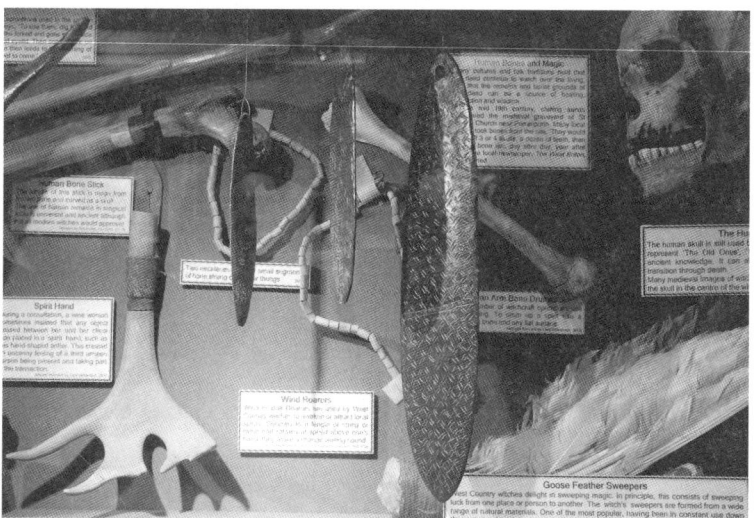

Above; a Bellarmine jug of the kind popularly employed as witch-bottles.
Below; a jar of pierced animal hearts displayed with other items of magical protection. Both from the Museum of Witchcraft

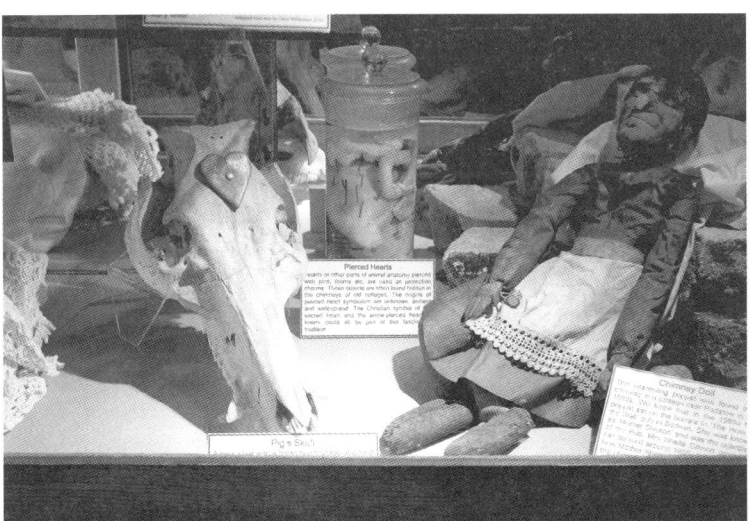

Above; a Caul or child's birth-cap. These membranes were, and still are, highly prized and sought-after by fisherman to be kept as charms of protection against drowning.
From the Museum of Witchcraft collection, Boscastle

*An example of a healing cage of bound twigs containing herbs and
substances of healing virtue.
From the Museum of Witchcraft collection, Boscastle*

Top; 'The Touch of the Dead' - a skeletal hand useful in the folk-magical healing artes.

Above; a healing bottle of hair and curative herbs with other items of magical healing. Both from the Museum of Witchcraft collection

Two plant charms for protection; a bunch of St John's Wort, and one of Dandelion flowers. Both are traditionally harvested and fashioned into charms at the magically potent time of midsummer.

Overleaf; a protective charm in the form of a roseary of hazelnuts.

All author's collection

Above; Footsep Magic - a lifted and carefully 'fenced in' footprint, used to exert a magical influence over the impression's maker.

Below; inscribed lead and nail charms.

Both from the Museum of Witchcraft collection

Lead from a Church Roof
Take lead from a church roof or window ,form a flattened strip, and scratch or engrave a spell on it. Roll it up and drive a nail through to seal the spell. Then, when the moon is right, bury it in a graveyard at night. These examples are from Blisland, Madron and St. Germans.

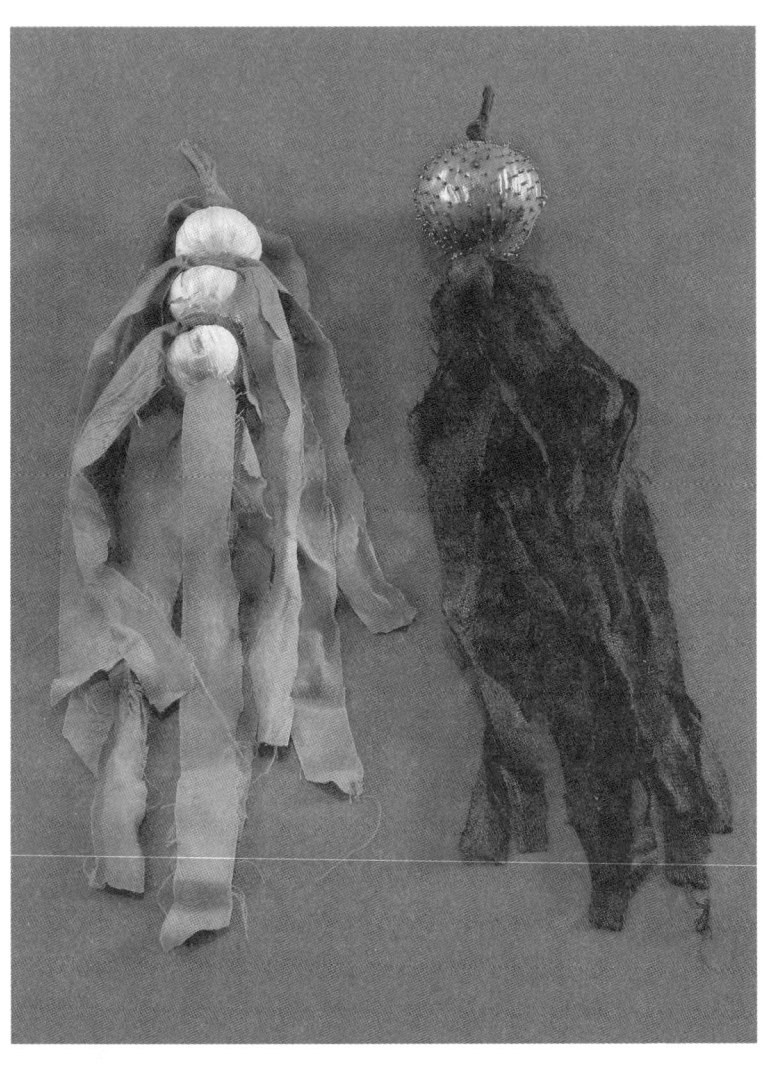

A protective charm of garlic-bulbs against the jealous or negative
attentions and influences of others,
and a counter-curse in the form of a pin-stuck onion.
Author's collection

Above; a logan or 'logging' stone on Zennor Hill, West Cornwall - a place of initiatory witch-rites by the potent spirit forces.

Below; St Buryan's churchyard - even today the location of West Cornish witch-rites of initiation and traditional magic

This dried toad is called Ben, and he was the "frog" spirit friend and guide of a Mrs Sarah Noakes of Crewkerne in the early 1920s. From the Museum of Witchcraft collection

The practitioner shall then remove from their fire two sticks, still burning and smoking at the ends, and these are crossed over the patient's wart whilst the charmer utters thrice;

'In the name of the Father Son and Holy Ghost I bid thee be gone!'

Wart Charming by the Moon - Upon first catching sight of the new moon, one may 'blow their warts away'. As the light of the moon grows to consume the dark, so shall the warts be consumed.

Conversely, a wart charming rite may be performed beneath a full moon, employing the waning virtue to remove the warts as it consumes the moon's light. The patient is taken outside under a clear full moon, and there shall the practitioner hold aloft their copper basin to charm into it the virtue of the moon. This is to be set before the kneeling patient who shall then 'wash' their hands within it with the following charm thrice repeated:

"I wash my hands in this thy dish,
O man in the moon, do grant my wish,
And come and take away this"

Touble-Bagging

Here follows an old West Country method for charming away from the patient all illnesses, curses, evil spirits, and diverse other maladies.

The practitioner shall have a square of sack cloth, and lay this out upon the ground. The patient is bid then to stand upon it so that the practitioner may 'look into them' for the evil. Once 'seen' the practitioner will charm the ill-influence downwards, with the left hand, drawing it down and out of the body of the patient, and out onto the cloth. The patient is then to step immediately off of it so that the practitioner may capture the evil by bagging and tying it within the sack cloth.

This is then to be taken to a crossroads; there to be buried at midnight.

For All Wounds, Injuries & Pains
The following magical square charm is to be inscribed and carried by the patient for the healing of sundry wounds and injuries;

H	A	P	P	I	R
A	M	A	O	S	I
P	A	R	A	O	P
P	O	A	R	A	P
I	S	O	A	M	A
R	I	P	P	A	H

Inscribe the following magical square to form a charm that shall be carried by the patient for relief from the suffering of all bodily pains;

For Burns

Upon visiting the charmer, the patient is instructed to gather nine bramble leaves, and bring these to the charmer who will put them into a vessel of water that has been drawn from a healing well.

Each leaf is then removed to be passed thrice by the charmer as they work over the afflicted part whilst uttering thrice the following charm;

> *"Three ladies came from the East,*
> *One with fire and two with frost;*
> *Out with thee fire, and in with thee frost! In the name of the*
> *Father, the Son, and the Holy Ghost, Amen."*

The practitioner will take then a burning stick from the hearth, and pass it over the afflicted part whilst repeating the same charm nine times. The charm spoken may also be inscribed to form a written charm for the patient to carry.

For Irritations and Eruptions of the Skin

The following charm may be said by the charmer over the afflicted part with passes of the hand, or the charmer's ashen staff. It may also be inscribed to form a written charm to be carried by the patient;

> *"Tetter, tetter, though hast nine sisters.*
> *God bless the flesh and preserve the bone,*
> *Perish thou tetter and be thou gone,*
> *In the name of the Father, Son and Holy Ghost, Amen!*
>
> *Tetter, tetter, though hast eight sisters.*
> *God bless the flesh and preserve the bone,*
> *Perish thou tetter and be thou gone,*
> *In the name of the Father, Son and Holy Ghost, Amen!"*

The reciting or inscribing of the charm is continued in reduction down to;

> *"Tetter, tetter, though hast no sisters.*
> *God bless the flesh and preserve the bone,*
> *Perish thou tetter and be thou gone,*
> *In the name of the Father, Son and Holy Ghost, Amen!"*

For Ulcers

For ulcers, the following magical square charm may be inscribed to form a written charm to be carried by the patient for a cure:

```
M E T S O R A H
E L M I N I M A
T M A R O M I R
S I R G I O N O
O N O I G R I S
R I M O R A M T
A M I N I M L E
H A R O S T E M
```

Against boils and blackheads

Take an elder twig two inches in length and a horseshoe nail. Insert the nail into the end of the twig and push it down through so that the point protrudes at the other end. The point must be cut off and the whole thing enclosed tightly by being sewn into white linen. The charm is to be worn about the neck of the sufferer, head upwards, until cured.

Against Bronchitis

A necklace of blue beads is provided to the sufferer to be worn as a curative charm.

Against Tonsillitis

A charm of red flannel is worn over the throat of the sufferer.

Against Fits

Where this affliction is divined to be the work of a black witch, the identity of the ill-wisher is sought by vision. The identification being made would allow the patient to be taken to the home of the one who has overlooked them, there shall glowing embers be taken from the witch's hearth and cast upon the floor so that the patient may be carried thrice over them. By this action would the evil influence be lifted.

Cure-Charms for Animals

Salt and a spoken charm are employed in this Exmoor rite for the general healing of cattle as an act of exorcising illness. Take to the animal a good amount of salt. Cast salt over the animal with the right hand, starting at the head working down the left side, or 'nearside', of the animal down to the tail. From there work back along the right or 'offside' of the animal, saying all the while the following charm;

"As thy servant Elishia healed the waters of Jericho
By casting the salt therein,
So I hope to heal this my beast,
In the Name of God the Father,
God the Son and God the Holy Ghost.
Amen."

To work a cure-charm for worm in a bullock's tongue, say over the animal the Lord's Prayer. Say then the following;

"When our blessed Lady set and sowed,
Her sweet son he set and played,

There come a tin-worm from the onder-wood
That stinged her swete son by the foot.
The bladder blawed, but didn't bust.
He that shall on thee call by his name Cobere,
In the name of the Father, and of the Son, and of the Holy Ghost."

Repeat again the Lord's Prayer and the charm is complete.

In the charming of Ringworm in cattle; the practitioner will work by encircling the sore three times against the sun as they charm for the affliction's demise, via its containment within the magical completion of its life-circle, and to impart curative influence upon the animal.

Desires and Good Fortune
✠

Moon Customs for Good Fortune

The West Country folk have long held faith in the ability of the moon to impart virtue, blessing and fecundity. There are preserved small and simple rites and taboos surrounding the moon, observed in order to ensure good fortune and its preservation.

Upon first catching sight of the new moon, one should turn money in one's pocket before curtseying three times to her. It is also fortunate to go outside and bathe in the virtue of the new moon. Tradition warns us though that to look upon the new moon, and the full, through glass is to be avoided as a bringer of ill-luck. In the event of this happening, the situation can be remedied by going outside in order to look at the moon over one's shoulder.

71

Pocket Charms for Good Fortune

To draw to one fortunate influences, various items may be carried as beneficent charms within the pocket according to West Country tradition. One such charm may be made by keeping the tip of a boiled cow's tongue, which should be preserved by allowing it to dry and carried to draw good fortune and luck.

The sensual snail has long been held to be a creature of fecund, potent, and blessed virtue, and their spiral form shells are desired charms. Most fortunate of all is a distinctly striped snail shell, which, upon finding, is to be immediately pocketed as a personal lucky charm.

It is quite understandable that the ancient and useful coal should be regarded as an amulet of good fortune, comfort and prosperity. This chthonic gift that fuels the fires of our progress and sustenance is to be kept in the coin purse as a charm for luck and prosperity, or else it is also fortunate, upon its finding, to spit upon the specimen before throwing it over one's right shoulder.

As a charm to guard against poverty, the following sign must be inscribed and carried within the pocket or within the purse:

The Toad Blessing

Upon taking residence in a new property, there is a West Country ritual employing the toad to make the new occupation a fortunate one.

A fine black (dark) toad is to be carried to the front door of the property and solemnly brought through the house and out of the rear door. Here, in the garden of the property, the creature is set free to dwell and care is given to seeing that its needs are met and comforts provided. The presence of the black toad will bestow blessings of good fortune upon the property and its inhabitants, as well as ensuring a fruitful garden.

Blessing by Grave Dust

The Cornish practitioner will visit the churchyard under the cover of night, and there, at the arrival of midnight, they shall gather grave dust within a properly conjured circle, and with the aid of the familiar spirits. The dust must then be baked within an iron vessel over a fire and, at its cooling, be ground finely into a powder. This is then to be placed to keep within a covered bowl, or a lidded box, and throughout all the operations of the substance's preparation, the virtues of blessing and fecundity are to be worked into it by will and by spirit. When called to the work of blessing, under a moon of increase, the practitioner may carry the vessel in a dextral circle about the item, creature, person, or place to receive the influence, casting all the while pinches of the grave dust to impart blessings of fecundity, good fortune, strength, and growth.

To Obtain One's Desires

From Somerset we have a charm, which may be inscribed and worn as well as recited, to obtain all that one desires:

"Sator, arepo, Tenet, opera, Rotas,
Jah, Jah, Jah,
Gnom Jah, Jah, Jah, Rethur,
Gehuvah, Siphereh, megach, Hod,
Yesod, Malkush, amalium,
Jouae, Juest, Shadrach,
Mislach, abedinego,
Be ye all present in my aid,
And for whatsoever I shall
Desire to obtain."

Fire Charms for the Desires of Love

To bring back an errant lover into the fold of the relationship, the client is to be instructed to go to their hearth where a good fire is to be lit. There, upon the hearth, a mixture is to be prepared of the Dragon's Blood resin, quicksilver, and of sulphur. This potent mixture is, upon the arrival of midnight, to be cast into the fire to conjure the lover's return.

The client desiring that their love for another is returned may be instructed to work the following charm at their hearth.

Upon cleaning and preparing a fish, remove and keep its heart. Cut from a piece of paper the shape of a heart and write upon it of your love. Take up the heart of the fish, and wrap it with care within the inscribed paper heart;

at every fold sticking it with a pin. This pin-stuck charm is then to be placed within the very hottest part of the hearth fire so that the one you desire shall feel for you the pricks of love.

Also for love, the following square may be inscribed, and speaking of those to be joined by its influence, the sign shall be enclosed within a small bag of silk to be carried by the one who desires the operation to come to fruition:

Vision
✠

Discovering a Thief

When approached to discover for a client the identity of a thief, via whichever methods of divination and sight the practitioner has preference for, the operation may be enhanced and aided greatly by the wearing of a Marigold charm.

Discovering Ill-Wishers and the Black Witch

For a client who seeks to have revealed unto them the identity of one who has placed upon them the influence of the ill-wish, they may be instructed to mount their horse and depart.

The reigns must be left loose so as not to influence the path of the beast in its motion, and let it proceed wherever it so pleases. Should the horse lead the enquirer to the door of some person's home, and there halt, the discovery has thus been made of the ill-wisher's dwelling.

The client whose cattle hath been bewitched may be instructed to perform the following rite to have revealed unto them the image of the 'black witch'. From the afflicted cattle, some blood is let to fall upon some straw. This straw is then to be set to burn upon the ground and the enquirer is to look for the image of the one who has overlooked their cattle appearing within the rising smoke issuing forth.

Oracle of Fire and Bay Leaves

For all endeavors, plans, situations and courses of action; the outcome being favorable or negative may be quickly divined at the hearth.

A handful of bay leaves is to be cast upon the hearth fire and watched intently. The fire's enthusiastic consuming of the leaves, crackling in the blaze, is an omen of good fortune and success. If however the leaves gently smolder and smoke in silence; it is an ill omen of failure and a warning of ill fortune.

To Obtain Wisdom from the Dead

Under the cover of night, the witch will make their way to the churchyard to find the grave of the one whose spirit they wish to interrogate for wisdom. There, at the arrival of midnight, the witch will walk nine times around the grave, muttering all the while they make their circumambulations in conjuration for the spirit to arise and give unto them the wisdom they seek.

Vision and Discoveries by the Squares

The practitioner wise in the artes of the squares may employ their aid within their oracular operations. The first square here given shall be worn beneath the practitioner's hat during their divinatory operations to know the past and present of matters;

Where the practitioner brings into employment such devices as magical mirrors, seeing glasses, 'shew stones' and crystals, the second square here shown may be placed so that the device is set upon it for the operation;

For operations in which the practitioner seeks to conjure forth visions within fire; the third square, here given above, shall be placed so that the flaming vessel may be set upon it, or else the square shall be placed before the fire.

For the conjurationn of oracular visions in water, the fourth square, here given below, shall be placed so that the vessel of water may be placed upon it, or else the square will be placed before the body of water employed;

Old Mother Green-Cap
✠
Plant Charms and Cures

O F all the verdant gifts of nature, unto the artes and Wort Cunning of the West Country 'Green Doctor' and 'Old Mother Green-Cap', the Ash tree is perhaps the most magically potent and reputable in West Country tradition; it is of great use for matters of protection, love, and the removal of diverse ills. Such is the power of the Ash, it is believed by employment of various methods to absorb or exorcise ailments and bewitchment.

An Ash Tree Rite against Toothache

To cure toothache, instruct the patient to visit an Ash tree; taking with them a good sharp knife. There they shall wrap their arms about the trunk of the tree, and make a slit within the bark within the point at which their hands meet. With the knife, the patient should cut some hair from the back of their head and secrete this beneath the bark of the tree via the slit made with the knife.

The Rite of the Cleft Ash

The mother of an ailing son must take him, with two virgin girls to assist the operation, to a young Ash tree. There the tree must

81

be split part way down its middle and the child placed by its mother into the cleft; there held for a moment before being taken by a virgin girl. The tree is then to be circled thrice against the sun. The virgin girl will then place the child to be held again in the cleft for a moment before the mother takes it and the circumambulations are again made about the tree. These actions are repeated nine times without any words being spoken throughout the operation, after which the split in the tree must be carefully closed together and bound to be revisited and inspected later. If the cleft grows together again, the child will grow strong and is healed.

For the healing of a girl child, the operation must be performed in the same manner by her father and two virgin boys.

A Fortunate Ash Charm

The leaves of the Ash may be plucked, and formed into a pleasing bunch. The gathered ends are to be bound tightly together in red, to form a foliate charm to be carried or hung in the home to attract love, good fortune, and health.

Protections by Ash

A stick of Ash has long been carried by walkers in the West Country to provide a protection against the adder or 'viper'. Kept in the home, by the door, the Ash stick performs the function of a protective charm to keep these venomous reptiles from entering.

A circle drawn with the Ash stick of a charmer about an adder will imprison the creature who will be unable to cross its boundary. An Ash tree growing in the garden will also provide like protection and keep adders away. In the absence of an Ash stick, the walker might carry leaves of the Ash within the pocket for a charm against the adder. The influence of the protective virtues of the Ash in West Country tradition of course extend beyond serpents to ward against the ill-wish. In Somerset, leafy Ash branches would be gathered and formed into a wreath to be hung from the tree growing nearest to the house. This wreath-charm would impart a protection upon the place from the influences of Black Witchcraft.

✠

Adder, Adder, Adder,
I lay under a stone
Or within a hole
He hath done this beast wrong

✠

The Virtues of Trees
✠

Alder
The Alder may be employed to provide protective and oracular virtues

Ash
The Ash is a potent and famed aid to all workings of healing and may be employed for acts of protection, curse lifting, love and divination.

Aspen
The Aspen is protective and healing in virtue. To cure fevers and ague a rite employing the aid of the Aspen may be performed thus: The Patient is to cut from their head a lock of hair which is to then be bound and nailed to the tree with these words;

"Aspen tree, Aspen tree,
I pray to thee
To shake and shiver instead of me."

Bay
The Bay is to be planted by thresholds to impart a protective influence upon the home, in addition to its leaves being bunched to hang inside the home as a charm for the same and for the blessings of good health.

The Bay is also of oracular virtue and is burned upon the hearth fire so that the behaviour of the leaves may be read. Placed beneath the pillow upon retiring for the night, it will induce good and prophetic dreams.

Birch

The protective virtues of the Birch may be harnessed by the presence of bunches of the tree's twigs which are kept to drive away evil spirits.

Blackthorn

The dark Blackthorn is of highly potent defensive virtues and an unrivalled aid to the work of blasting or 'Owl Blinking'. The West Country Wise folk will also harness the Blackthorn's virtues and potency for blessing, fertility and power.

Elder

The Elder is in Cornwall known as 'Lady Elder'. The Elder's influence may be employed to provide a protection for horses by the hanging of her branches within stables and above their doors. Protections may likewise be imparted upon the home by the fixing of bunches of Elder leaves to the doors and the windows. Thus is formed a Cornish charm against ill-wishing and the influence of the black witch.

A tree also of the Faery Folk, the Elder must not be burnt, for such a taboo act is sure to invite ill-influence from the spirit world. The ripe berries of the Elder are good for phlegm and for the sinuses.

Hawthorn

Another tree of the Faery Folk; the Hawthorn must not be burnt. The West Country practitioner will perform acts of magic beneath the overarching wind-distorted Hawthorn that call upon the aid of the Faery Folk; especially for matters of protection. After such acts, offerings of food and drink must be made.

The Hawthorn is heavily associated with the coming of summer, the arrival of its 'May' blossoms being watched for as the traditional sign. In Cornwall, folk would visit a Hawthorn tree for celebratory May Day rites in which the tree is bedecked with candles and danced around joyously. The Hawthorn, however, does not make a good walking stick, for West Country lore holds that it will invite ill-fortune upon journeys.

Hazel
The Hazel may be employed within rites and workings for wisdom, divination, and dowsing. It is employed also within traditional curative rites against the bites of the adder and other 'stinging' creatures.

Holly
The formidable Holly is understandably protective in virtue. It is hung from the door-handles as a Cornish charm for the protection of the home. The Holly is particularly protective against lightening; the influence being enjoyed by places both where it is installed in the form of a charm, and where the living Holly grows.

Ivy
The strong Ivy is of highly useful restrictive, binding and protective virtue. The climbing Ivy, grown up the walls of the cottage, creates a verdant shell of protection around the home.

Rowan
The Rowan, or 'Care', is of quickening virtue for all tasks and potently protective. To form a Cornish charm of personal protection, the red berries of the Rowan may be threaded and worn as a necklace. To impart protections upon the home, the Rowan may be planted near doorways, and in some Cornish cottages, the crossbeam of the fire is made of rowan wood in order to prevent evil entering the home via the chimney. To impart a potent protection on the home for the year; branches of the Rowan are to be hung over doorways on May morning. A farm near Castle

Cary in Somerset, still by the early 1960s, held such faith in the protective virtues of the Rowan that bunches of the tree's twigs were collected and tied with red thread above the doors of the farmhouse, the cow shed, the chicken coop and the pig sty. These charms were installed on May's Eve and on Hallows' Eve – two of the three 'spirit nights' of the year – "to keep the faeries and black witches at bay". [1]

Infusions of Virtue
✠

Both the wild hedge-row, and the working garden, provide the green-doctor with highly virtuous wort whose potencies may not only be employed within the creation of charms, or for burning to issue forth their powers within magical rites and workings. These gifts may also be made great use of to prepare potent infusions to give their virtue, aid and strength unto the needs of body, mind, and the spirit.

Here follow but some of the various wort and their virtues enjoyed within West Country infusions;

Bramble Leaves
The Leaves of the Bramble, or Blackberry, are good for the treating of cankers or ulcers in the mouth and the throat.
Camomile
The Camomile is good for the soothing aching stomachs, for ulcers and for the pains of teething.
Elderberry
The ripe Elderberry is good against phlegm and for the suffering sinuses.

Elderflower

The Elderflower is good for relief from fevers, and with honey it is good for chills.

Melissa

The Melissa, or Lemon Balm, is good for the treatment of depression, attacks of anxiety, and for the circulation.

Mugwort

The Mugwort is good for colds of the head.

Nettle

The Nettle is good for the digestive system and works against pleurisy and infections of the throat.

Pennyroyal

The Pennyroyal makes an elixir to be drunk for enlivening of the spirit and against fatigue.

Periwinkle

An infusion of the Periwinkle will encourage passions and love within those who partake of it.

Rosemary

Infusions of the Rosemary should be applied to the scalp to ward against hair loss and to encourage strong re-growth. Some say that the potency of this infusion is enhanced greatly by collecting the water to be employed from the hollows in the roots of great Beech Trees.

Sage

Infusions of the potent Sage should be drunk regularly for good health, long life, and to ward off lethargy.

Thyme

The Thyme is good for the treatment of sore throats, headaches and insomnia.

Valerian

The Valerian creates an infusion that will draw love unto its drinker.

Curative Plant Charms
✠

Wart Charming by Wort

Gather fresh the Groundsel, and rub the juice of this upon each wart possessed by the patient. Hand this plant then to the patient who is to be instructed to throw it backwards over their head, and not to look back after it. Then shall the charmer bury the plant in the spot where it lands. As the Groundsel does rot; so shall fade the warts.

Gather from the Gooseberry, one prickle for each wart upon the client's body. Stick each prickle well into their wart. When each wart has been stuck, the charmer shall gather the prickles and bury them.

Harvest a fresh stick of Hazel, and into the length of this stick cut a notch with a good clean knife; one notch being cut for each wart possessed by the client. Touch then each notch thrice unto their corresponding wart, before giving the stick to the client; being instructed to take it at midnight to a crossroads and there to be buried.

The Bramble Arch

To charm away sundry ailments, take the patient to a good length of Bramble that has taken root at both ends, so that its midst may be lifted up to form an arch of sufficient height that a person may pass under by crawling. Have there the patient pass in such a manner thrice beneath the Bramble arch against the sun to diminish the influence of the ailment.

Against Rheumatism

A Potato is to be obtained, and it must be one that has been stolen. This is to be kept on the person of the patient by carrying it in the pocket as a charm to ward against the pains of Rheumatism.

Against the Shingles

There are two rites employing Rushes and the arte of the circle that the Charmer may perform for the client afflicted with the shingles.

For this operation, the charmer shall gather some Rushes, upon receiving the patient; the charmer shall work the Rushes into a circlet to be placed for a moment over the ailing part of their client. The charmer shall then remove the circlet and hang it up within their chimney. This ritual is to be repeated three times, with the charmer having harvested a new handful of Rushes upon each occasion.

For the second method, the charmer is again to gather Rushes to employ upon their client's visit. The charmer shall then take the Rushes in hand, and will circumambulate the patient, carrying the Rushes and charming the ailment as they go. This rite, like the former, is to be observed upon three occasions, again with fresh Rushes being harvested by the charmer each time.

Against the Scrofula

Dig up with care the Vervain so that its root may be harvested and prepared. Enclose the root within a sewn white bag to be worn about the neck of the patient as a charm against the Scrofula.

Against Weakness of the Eyes

In Cornish practice, the patient is brought to the hearth of the charmer, who will have there some thorny lengths of the Bramble. These are held so in the hearth-fire by the charmer that their ends will ignite. Withdrawn from the fire, the charmer will then wave the smouldering and smoking Bramble lengths in front of the patient's eyes, exorcising their weakness as they charm.

Against Ringworm

An ointment is to be prepared of Pennyroyal and lard. This is to be applied on three occasions to the ailment; upon each application the charmer will encircle thrice the afflicted area against the sun.

To Stop Bleeds of the Nose

Gather the Periwinkle to be held in the mouth of the patient suffering from bleeding from the nose, and therein to be held until the bleed has stopped.

Three Hazelwood Rites to Charm the Adder Bite
Cut a good slender length of Hazelwood, cutting this again
in two parts which are to be together bound into the form
of a cross. Lay gently this cross upon the bite and charm
forcefully thrice with the following words:

"Underneath this hazelin mote
There's a Braggoty worm with a speckled throat,
Nine double is he:
Now from nine double to eight double,
And from eight double to seven double,
And from seven double to six double,
And from six double to five double,
And from five double to four double,
And from four double to three double,
And from three double to two double,
And from two double to one double,
And from one double to no double,
No double hath he!"

To employ another method, a slender length of Hazel is
to be cut and twisted into a ring large enough to be placed
over the head of the patient.

Yet another method, which is held to cure the stings and
bites of insects as well as those of the adder, demands that
nine shots of Hazel be cut. The charmer is to strike with
these the wound three times, with each strike repeating the
first verse of the sixty eighth Psalm:

"let God arise, let His enemies be scattered: let them also that hate
him flee before him."

For Good Hair Growth

Warm Oil of Tartar and rub it lightly into a balding place to make hair grow. Also, for the patient suffering thinning of the hair, the practitioner may harvest some good lengths of Ivy and from these form a wreath-crown. This is to be worn by the patient against further hair loss and to encourage strong new growth of the hair.

Against Fatigue

The Mugwort is a kind ally to the traveller. A little is to be harvested fresh to be placed inside the shoes as a charm to ward off fatigue when one is walking, and with the Mugwort's influence, the journey will feel as though it is only half of its actual length.

Protective Plant Charms
✠

Against the Black Witch

The following plant substances are particularly notable for their virtues of protection against the presence, attentions and influence of the black witch, whilst plants possessed of other specific protective virtues as well as those of a more general and all-encompassing protective virtue, shall be given here also.

Our plant world allies against the powers of the black witch include the pungent Asafoetida, Dill, Elder, Hazelnuts, Meadowsweet, Rowan, St John's Wort, Trefoil (symbolic of the Holy Trinity), Valerian, Vervain and the Woody Nightshade. To employ the virtues of these materials of nature, one may incorporate them into personal charms to be carried by the recipient of the protections, or fashion them into plant-charms to be installed around the home and property of the recipient; most suitably within or above the portal points of the home – the windows, doors, the hearth and inside the chimney – where they may exert their influence against the maleficia of the black witch in the very places such evil might seek to make its entry.

A note regarding the binding together of herbs, flowers and plants into bunches; either as charms or otherwise: many years ago in Penzance I heard an elderly Cornish woman warning a florist, who sold flowers bound together in bunches with sisal twine, that to do so was a very unlucky thing. Flowers and herbs, she advised, should be bunched by tying them with gay ribbons, and never with twine or string. She returned later with much shiny blue ribbon for the young florist to use instead, saying to him "the Cornish should always help the Cornish". Out of politeness he accepted the ribbon, but had no intention of using it as the sisal twine produced the 'rustic' appearance he was after. I'm sad to report that the young florist was far from fortunate thereafter; he suffered much financial hardship and lost his second child to miscarriage before finally losing his business.

When affixed above the door, as with the horseshoe, protective plant charms are a powerful visual sign and warning to the minds of all those who see it, or pass beneath it upon entry, that the property is under the protection of a potent magical nature. To those who are the owners or tenants of the building in question; be it a home or outbuilding, such charms instil confidence as a constant comfort and reminder. Yet, as we see with magical chimney installations, positioning in plain sight is by no means necessary to the efficacy of the material used as a protective charm. The above mentioned materials may also be gathered for enclosure and sealing within a bottle-vessel, most suitably of glass or salt-glazed stoneware; both being materials traditionally attributed with magical protective virtues themselves. This vessel, once prepared, may be interred beneath the threshold, or beneath the hearth. As well as working again within major portal points, the ritual act of magical burial is to make the charm part of the very building; imbuing the whole with its protective virtue.

Asafoetida

The Asafoetida, a substance named also Devil's Dung for the offensiveness of its pungent odour, provides a potent aid in its burning within rites and workings for the lifting of the black witch's ill-influence, and for the exorcism of evil spirits.

Dandelion

Upon Midsummer's Eve, gather a good number of large and bright Dandelion flowers. Bind them into bunches to be hung in the doors and windows of the home as a powerful charm against all ill influence.

Elder

The Elder may be employed to form a Cornish Charm against ill-wishing. Gather the leaves of the Elder into bunches, and fix these with an iron nail to the doors and the window frames of the building to be protected from the influence of the black witch.

Hazelnuts

Gather fifty-nine good Hazelnuts and pierce each one through so that they may be threaded into the form of a Rosary, terminating in a tassel of red. This charm is to be hung within the home to provide protection from the ill-wishing of the black witch.

Meadowsweet

Gather and fashion the Meadowsweet into garlands, and install these about the home and outbuildings to guard against ill-wishing.

Mistletoe

The sacred Mistletoe, brought into the home for the midwinter festivities, should remain in place all the year to hang as a protective charm, and one that will encourage peace within the home. It is protective also from lightening and a charm to guard against poverty.

Rosemary

It is wise indeed to have Rosemary growing in the garden, and to keep it fashioned into charms to hang within the home as a potent plant-charm; protective against all evil spirits and calamity. Such a presence brings also good fortune, success in enterprise, and attracts love to the individual who carries it.

Rowan

The Rowan is a most potent protection against ill-wishing; both in the form of personal charms and household protections. For either use, both the prepared twigs and the red berries may be employed, traditionally together with red thread. Small bound crosses of Rowan twigs and the threaded berries may be carried as pocket charms, or hung within the home at the portal points. As we have seen, the Rowan's berries would in Cornwall be threaded to form protective necklaces, and the tree's planting near doorways imparts upon the building a protective virtue to avert the power of the black witch and evil spirits, as does the ritual affixing of red thread bound Rowan branch and twig bunches above doorways upon the potent eves of May and November.

Valerian

Enclose the Valerian within a charm bag to be worn as protection against lightening and the black witch's ill-wishing.

Vervain

The Vervain enclosed within a charm bag may be worn round neck of the client, upon retiring to bed, to provide a protection against bad dreams.

Woody Nightshade

The Woody Nightshade may be fashioned into charms, both to be worn and for installation within buildings, to provide a protection against all ill-wishing and evil influences. For a patient suffering from the attentions of the black witch, the practitioner may form a crown-wreath of the Woody Nightshade. Place it upon the patient's head during rites to exorcise the ill-influence.

Yarrow

Have the Yarrow strewn upon the threshold of the home to ward against the entry of any evil influence. The Yarrow may also be fashioned into a charm to be hung within the home on St John's Eve; it will provide a protection for the home all year against illness.

Plant Protections for Babes

To keep evil spirits away, gather Cowslip and bind it into a bunch to be hung as a protective charm above the crib. The Chamomile may likewise be fashioned into a charm and hung above the crib to keep illness away. Branches of the potent Ash were placed beneath the cribs of newborn babes to prevent the Good Folk from stealing them away to the Otherworld. Cots were also sometimes made from Ash wood for its protective virtue.[2]

Plant Charms for Love
✠

Dragon's Blood Love Spell

The client desiring to have the one they love shall be provided, by the practitioner, with the precious and magically potent red tree resin; Dragons' Blood. A copper vessel is required also for the spell the client is to be instructed to perform at their hearth. At midnight, upon a Friday and under the growing of the moon, the client must remove burning coals from the hearth fire, and place these within the copper vessel. Upon these coals, the client must then scatter the Dragon's Blood resin to burn. Over the rising smoke as it issues forth from the copper vessel, the client must say;

"Tis not this Dragon's Blood I mean to burn, but my true love's heart I wish to turn. May he have no sleep, nor rest, nor pleasure see, until that he comes back to me. So shall it be!"

Valerian Love Charm

For the client who wishes to have love attracted unto them, the practitioner may create a personal charm employing the Valerian. A small square bag of white is made, and within this is the Valerian enclosed and sewn shut. The charm is provided to the client to be worn about the neck.

Laurel Love Bindings

Lovers, who wish to keep strong their love and guard it safe from all adverse intrusions, may be instructed each to have a Laurel twig. Each must break in two their twig, and with each other exchange one half. Both shall then bind their two halves together to be kept as a charm and token to protect and keep strong their love.

The client who wishes to have returned unto them an errant lover may be instructed to employ Laurel leaves, in a manner similar to that of the Dragon's Blood Love Spell. Here, the leaves are to be burnt at the hearth, using the same words but beginning instead;

"Tis not these leaves I mean to burn, but my true love's heart I wish to turn...etc"

Blackthorn Blessing Ash
✠

One may be quite justifiably tempted to regard the virtues of the Blackthorn, growing prolifically as it does in these parts to form stark and formidable thorny boundaries atop the hedges of field and lane, and dark impenetrable thickets within the wooded un-worked valleys and dips of land, as being of use principally within the areas of defensive and offensive magics of blasting and retribution. However, the qualities possessed by the Blackthorn are inclusive of invulnerability, pertinacity, fecund growth, abundance and prolific progress, and these are all of course blessings of a highly desirable nature.

Thus, when the practitioner is called to impart blessings upon land, buildings, people or animals; the Blackthorn Blessing Ash may be prepared and employed with much efficacy.

Upon a night of the full moon, the practitioner will work the rites using a staff of Blackthorn to form their Circle of Arte, and at its centre, where the ways are crossed, a blessed fire is built of thorny twigs and branches of the Blackthorn. This fire is fed and maintained, with the practitioner making circumambulations about it; chanting and charming into it the blessed virtues desired, until all is transformed into ash. The Blackthorn ashes are to be gathered and ground into the finest of powders, all the while with the practitioner's mind firmly fixed on the virtues, working these into the preparation, as was done with the fire.

A suitable stoppable or covered vessel must be found into which the powder is transferred for keeping, and for taking to the place of working when it is to be employed.

When the powder is required, the practitioner will pace about the land, building, item, person, or animal with the open vessel in a sun-wise direction. As they go, the practitioner will all the while scatter with the right hand the powder toward the object, until it is felt the blessed virtues have been suitably imparted.

Plant Charms for Animals
✠

Averting illness, the influence of ill-wishing, and the unwanted attentions of spirits from cattle and horses, has long been of vital concern to country folk. In the West Country, to provide such protections, plants of virtue have long been formed into wreath-charms.

The Rowan, or 'Care', in addition to being affixed above the doorways to animal shelters as a protection, is also fashioned into wreaths to be placed about the stalls, and about the horns of cattle to lift the influences of the black witch's ill-wish and the unwanted attentions of spirits. Such charm-wreaths will guard also against any future intrusions of a magical or otherworldly nature, or as a preventative.

The Woodbine, or 'hare' and the Woody Nightshade, the latter as we have seen being employed for humans also, are both plants that have traditionally been twisted into collar wreaths to be placed about the necks of cattle to ward off malign influences and ill-wishing. To the Woody Nightshade is added Holly; forming a collar-charm which is held to provide a potent protection for horses.

When an animal has fallen ill, wreathing it with the Rowan has been held in the West Country to prevent the animal's illness getting worse. When the 'foot and mouth' disease was found to be present within animals, the condition was not overreacted to in the slightest or with the same level of panic and hysteria that it is today. Simple remedies and cures were employed, and again we find the use of the Ash tree's potent healing virtues; for Ash leaves were once fed to cattle as a cure for this relatively mild complaint.

1 & 2. Shared by Michael Howard via personal correspondence.

Old Mother Black-Cap

✠

Owl-Blinking and Turning

N acceptance that the traditional magical practitioner is possessed of the ability to cure, to bless, and to charm, should quite naturally lead one to the conclusion that there is another side to the coin, and that such people are possessed also of the power, when necessity arises, to inflict magical harm and retaliation, or cursing, blasting, and 'turning'.

Some have gone to great lengths to draw a clear distinction between the 'black' and the 'white' practitioner; being the exclusively malevolent 'witch', as distinct from the entirely benevolent 'wise-woman' and the 'cunning-man' who work only to destroy the influence of the former. In some areas such distinctions may have some accuracy, but here in the West Country, such distinctions are very difficult indeed to make. One may hear in the West Country of 'white witches' and 'black witches', but in truth they are one in the same. Whether a West Country witch is 'white' or 'black' depends entirely on the nature of your relationship with their craft; whether you are a client seeking their aid, or one who has wronged the client. Thus to the client consulting a practitioner for magical retribution against a wrongdoer; the witch is 'white', yet in the very same instance to the recipient of the working; the witch is most definitely 'black'. Thus we see that one who is of the 'true breed' of Cornish and West Country witch is known as a 'Double Ways' practitioner.

Here then we come to the darker ways of the West Country practitioner's arte; for their abilities to cure, bless and charm are indeed balanced by their twin powers of cursing and magical retaliation. In the West Country, the practice of cursing is known as 'Owl Blinking' or 'Owl Blasting', and magical retaliation against an ill-wisher, which is not only defensive, but often deliberately offensive in nature, is known as 'Counter-Blasting' or 'Turning'.

Curse-Magic and Blasting
✠

Footstep Magic

Much of traditional magic relies on the obtaining of a connection or 'magical link' with the object of the working, allowing the practitioner to win influence over the target of their work. These conduits of connection; be they the knots touched to warts, or bodily substances collected by stealth and incorporated into a poppet or magical likeness, may be employed by the practitioner to exert their will and influence for either beneficent or malefic results. Footstep magic is no exception, and is a very potent method for establishing a magical link as a tool for 'double-ways' working, and may be employed for the purposes of healing; to 'pin down' and diminish an ailment via an iron nail and the footstep made at the moment of the ailment's attack. However, the particular method here to be described would tend to be more often employed for malefic intent.

The footstep, or footprint, is a most personal mark; it is the mark of one's path through life, and a trail left behind that may be followed magically, like fire along gunpowder. The boot that leaves the mark bares the scars of every step its owner has made in them, thus being a good part of the reason why shoes and boots are often found concealed within the fabric of houses as a folk-magical decoy for any maleficia directed towards their owner, much in the same manner as a bottle filled with hair, nail parings and bodily fluids.

If a good footprint left by an individual to be worked upon can be found, then a practitioner can have a potent influence over them.

With great care, the footprint must be lifted, and removed to the practitioner's place of working. Here, thread and pin magic are employed to contain and secure the magical link with the footprint's maker. The footprint is skilfully fenced in by use of such things as pins, thorns, small sticks or matches, to 'pin down' the essence of the target of the working.

The act of pinning is also magically symbolic of the injection of will or influence. These 'fence-posts' are then carefully woven round and around with thread; an act of binding the strand of fate and future life path of the individual unto the influence of the practitioner, be it for good or for ill, and via whichever methods are most suited to the results desired.

This is not a working of brevity, but one in which, via the keeping of the fenced-in footstep is to be worked slowly and carefully executed over a long period of time.

The Lead and Nail Spell

Another method of working that may be employed for a variety of needs, for good or for ill; is the lead and nail spell, although it, like footstep magic, may more usually have been employed for the execution of a curse.

It is again a spell intended to last and to work over a long period of time, and thus the immortal lead is employed. It calls upon the aid of chthonic force and an iron nail, representing the will of the practitioner, is employed to 'pin down' the magic and to exert the magical influence over the target of the working.

A sheet of lead is to be obtained which, it is said, will be all the more potent if it has been stolen from the roof or windows of a church. A hammer and a good iron nail are required also, and these are to be taken, under the cover of midnight, to a churchyard. Here, in the area outside the north door, the Circle of arte is to be worked, and a small hole dug before the chthonic force is raised by circumambulation and low chanting.

Kneeling before the hole, and by the light of a single lantern, the iron nail is taken in hand to inscribe the words of intent, along with any pertinent signs, into the sheet of lead, all the while with the intent of the working being muttered over it.

The lead sheet is then to be rolled up, with the inscribed side being innermost, and placed within the hole. The hammer and the nail are then to be taken up, and the nail held point downward over the roll of lead. As the words of intent are uttered a final time, the nail is struck right through the lead; pinning it to the ground. The hole is filled in; being mindful to replace the turf and take every care to ensure no visual signs are left of the ground having been disturbed, lest your spell be discovered.

As he loved cursing,
so let it come unto him:
as he delighted not in blessing,
so let it be far from him.

✠

The Parsley and the Cursing Psalm
In West Country tradition, the Parsley is quite possessed of
an evil reputation, thus it may be employed within magical
workings of malefic intent. Within all such workings and
rites, the parsley may be burnt whilst the curses and words

of malediction are uttered into the rising smoke as it issues forth. Within Cornish magical tradition, all workings of blasting against enemies and wrongdoers are aided by the employment of the 109th Psalm:

"Hold not thy peace, O God of my praise; for the mouth of the wicked and the mouth of the deceitful are opened against me: they have spoken against me with a lying tongue. They compassed me about also with words of hatred; and fought against me without a cause. For my love they are my adversaries: but I give myself unto prayer. And they have rewarded me evil for good, and hatred for my love. Set thou a wicked man over him: and let Satan stand at his right hand. When he shall be judged, let him be condemned: and let his prayer become sin. Let his days be few; and let another take his office. Let his children be fatherless, and his wife a widow. Let his children be continually vagabonds, and beg: let them seek their bread also out of their desolate places. Let the extortioner catch all that he hath; and let the strangers spoil his labour. Let there be none to extend mercy unto him: neither let there be any to favour his fatherless children. Let his posterity be cut off; and in the generation following let their name be blotted out. Let the iniquity of his fathers be remembered with the Lord; and let not the sin of his mother be blotted out. Let them be before the Lord continually, that he may cut off the memory of them from the earth. Because that he remembered not to shew mercy, but persecuted the poor and needy man, that he might even slay the broken in heart. As he loved cursing, so let it come unto him: as he delighted not in blessing, so let it be far from him. As he clothed himself with cursing like as with his garment, so let it come into his bowels like water, and like oil into his bones. Let it be unto him as the garment which covereth him, and for a girdle wherewith he is girded continually. Let this be the reward of mine adversaries from the Lord, and of them that speak evil against my soul. But do thou for me, O God the Lord, for thy

name's sake: because thy mercy is good, deliver thou me. For I am poor and needy, and my heart is wounded within me. I am gone like the shadow when it declineth: I am tossed up and down as the locust. My knees are weak through fasting; and my flesh faileth of fatness. I became also a reproach unto them: when they looked upon me they shaked their heads. Help me, O Lord my God: O save me according to thy mercy: That they may know that this is thy hand; that thou, Lord, hast done it. Let them curse, but bless thou: when they arise, let them be ashamed; but let thy servant rejoice. Let mine adversaries be clothed with shame, and let them cover themselves with their own confusion, as with a mantle. I will greatly praise the Lord with my mouth; yea, I will praise him among the multitude. For he shall stand at the right hand of the poor, to save him from those that condemn his soul."

To Summon a Curse

The Cornish witch, when seeking to conjure vengeful spirit forces and curses upon an enemy or wrongdoer, might take themselves to walk along the winding paths of the towering sea cliffs, climbing to the highest rocky outcrop. The witch shall have with them a horn, and here, looking out over the sea with their working staff in hand, the witch will conjure forth power from the darkest parts of the tumultuous 'well of emotion', and the black spirits of the wind to convey their will. The words of intent are cried out and the horn blown to summon the curse and send it forth to descend upon its quarry.

For the Punishment of an Unfaithful Lover

One must buy a new candle and its price must not be haggled over. Take the candle to the hearth with three pins, and at midnight light the candle. Heat then the point of each pin within the flame before sticking them into the candle whilst uttering the following words: *"Thrice is the candle broke by me, and thrice thy heart shall broken be."*

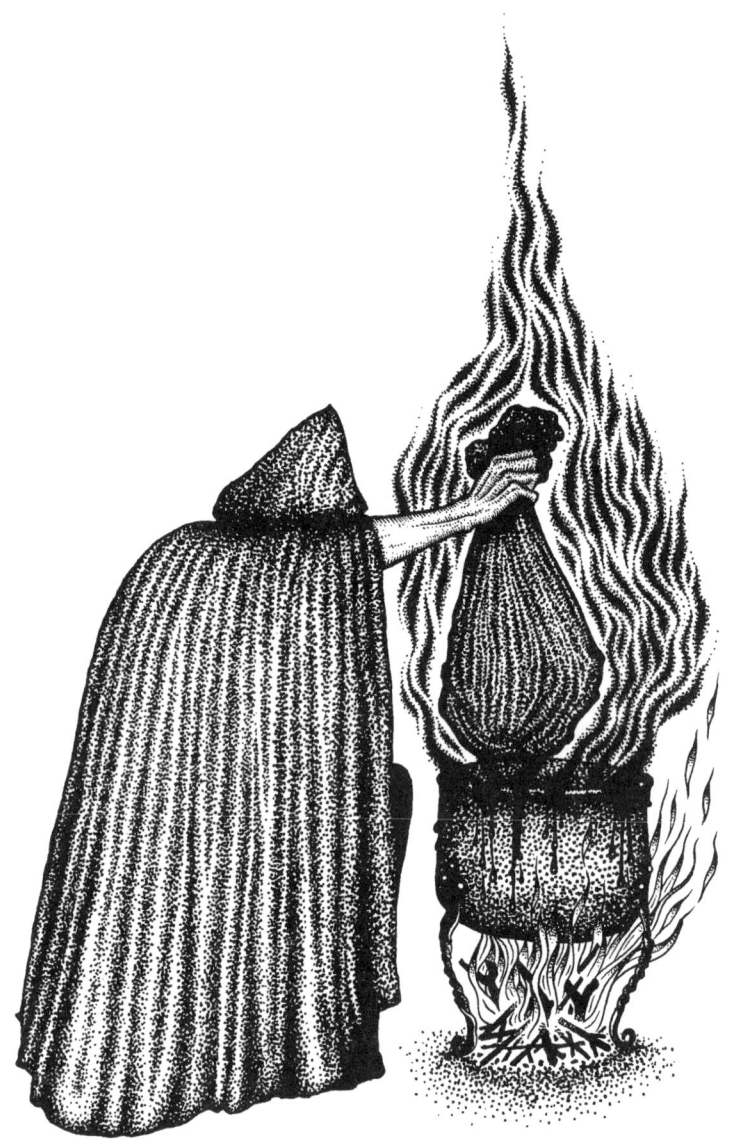

An Ill-Wishing Bag

Here we come to a working of true West Country 'black witchcraft' intended to bring ill-fortune and disaster upon a person; pervading their life, work and home. To perform it, a draw-string bag of sacking material is to be made. In great secrecy, the witch must visit the property of the victim, and into the bag must be placed a little something from everything that is owned by them and is of their life and work. In the case of a farmer, for example, we are told that the witch must place such things in the bag "as a feather from the cockerels, hair from the cows etc., even nuts and bolts from the tractors, corn grinders, carts, etc." (From the magical notes of Cecil H. Williamson)

The witch will then remove the curse-bag to their place of working, and there prepare the Circle of Arte with a large iron cauldron of molten tar, bubbling over a fire. The bag is held aloft the cauldron and at great length and in great detail are curses against the victim spoken over the bag as it is lowered into the black tar, and there left for some set time. When the witch has determined the time is right, the curse-bag is lifted out of the molten tar, and hung in some place to dry and harden. When it is ready, the hardened curse-bag is taken, again in great secrecy, back to the property, and there it is to be well hidden, behind a roof timber being a favourite place for such things, and left to work its baneful influence.

To Curse an Enemy

To inflict a slow, yet terrible wasting curse upon an enemy, the witch shall collect much soot; the charm will be all the more efficacious if the soot can be gathered from the fire-back and chimney of the victim of this baneful work.

The witch shall begin to make a modest loaf of bread, which shall be blackened by the soot being added to the mixture. As the dough is worked, the witch shall have their mind firmly fixed upon the victim and the things they are to suffer as a result of the curse; muttering and 'working' these things into the dough.

When it is ready to be baked, the witch shall hold aloft the loaf and in the Old One's name they shall 'Christen' it with the name of the victim; marking their initials upon it before it is put into the oven. The witch shall then take up a good large knife; marking it upon the hilt with the name of the one who has been wronged by the one to be cursed, and in the Old One's name it also is so 'Christened'.

When the curse-loaf is ready, and whilst it is still quite warm, the witch will hold the knife above it and pronounce over the loaf the curse that is to fall upon the wrongdoer as the knife is plunged deep into it. The knife-stuck curse-loaf is then to be taken by the witch to some secret, dark and damp place, and there it shall be hung up and left. As the loaf disintegrates by mildew and rot, so shall the victim of the curse suffer greatly.

To Kill an Enemy

The witch, by stealth, shall carefully go about gathering things of the victim; intimate and personal in nature. Such things as nail parings, hair removed from their brush or comb, threads and pieces of fabric torn from their clothing – undergarments that are unwashed being the most potent magical link of this sort – table scraps from their meals, soot or ash from their fire, earth taken from the middle of their footprint, and anything else intimately linked with the victim the witch is able to gather over a period of time.

When the collection is thought complete, the things are together bound and mixed into a viscid mixture of baneful herbs and flour paste. This execrable mass is bound round and around with string; fixing it to a stick which has been prepared especially for the working. At either end of the stick, lengths of string are affixed, and at the ends of these are two holed flint 'hag-stones' tied.

Upon a suitably unpleasant night, the witch will journey out; taking the curious device to a lonely large old oak tree. There, the device in hand, shall the witch make lengthy sinistral circumambulations and dances around the tree, all the while making dark incantations of the victim's fate. At the rite's climax, the witch shall stop; throwing the device with a shriek up as high into the tree as can be mustered. There shall the thing be left to be torn at and destroyed by the elements, to bring a wasting death upon the one it represents

A Square for Black Spells

When it is found that a person is deserving of the practitioner's influences of ill-intent, then the magical square here given shall be inscribed and taken by stealth to be buried beneath the pathway to the victim's door, or else some other path they are known to walk. Whatever spot is chosen, it must be one over which the victim passes upon a regular basis. This done, the practitioner will now be able to cast upon the person any black spells of punishment of their choosing.

Retaliation Magic and Counter-Blasting
✠

Charms and magical rites to torment and destroy the power of the black witch, it is to be found, will most often employ metal (particularly iron), or fire, or in some cases both metal and fire. It was an old, famed and trusted method in the West Country and elsewhere, employed commonly until alarmingly recently, to draw the black witch's blood.

Such ferrous implements as needles, pins, nails and knives have traditionally been used to cause a suspected witch to bleed, and particularly to 'score' the witch 'above the breath'. Here, the suspected black witch is attacked, often with some brutality, and usually by the one who believes their self to be bewitched, and stabbed at, cut or torn upon the brow so that their blood may be let forth. Contained within this practice are ancient beliefs surrounding witch-blood as a vessel of magical power, the breath as a vehicle via which the witch may send forth her magical will, and the protective virtues of iron against maleficia. The attacker acts also above the witch's eyes, well known also cross-culturally as traditional conveyors of witch power, and the mouth that shapes the words of malediction and cursing (or blessing and healing) and gives manifestation unto the witch's will.

The witch's spittle, as we have seen, is also a vehicle of power for good or for ill. Thus by cutting, usually in the form of the cross, above these things, and by the witch having her blood spilt by a non-witch, it was believed she would lose her powers and have no further magical influence.

Fire, as well as being anciently employed to make magic, is employed traditionally also to break or 'lift' it. We have seen that passing through or over fire; especially in the case of the victim being passed over fire taken from the hearth of the black witch, are traditional means of lifting from one the influence of the witch's curse. Passing fire over the black witch is another West Country method employed to achieve the same result; throwing a shovel-full of burning 'ummers' (embers) over the witch would lift the curse and destroy her influence.

Image magic, and the use of 'poppets' or 'fith-faths' are, like fire, not the exclusive domain of the witch (who in popular thought employs such devices purely for the work of cursing, but in reality more often than not for curing), but may traditionally be employed by the victim against the black witch, usually under the instruction of another practitioner learned in the ways of cursing and dark magic.

Some might be instructed to form an effigy in the likeness of the evil-doer, and then to pierce the thing through with a long pin. To others it may be specified that the likeness must be crafted from wax, and then left before the fire to slowly melt away. Sometimes this effigy must first be stuck full with many pins prior to its melting. In both cases, it is intended that as the likeness melts slowly away, so shall the black witch's power (and possibly her life) fade away into nothing.

The inclusion of pins within the rite would be intended to inflict additional suffering, by stabbing and pricking at the black witch. The act of sticking the black witch's likeness with pins might also be held to be a means of 'turning' the maleficia she had inflicted upon her victim back upon herself with interest; the greater the number of pins the greater the rebound. Here we must also be mindful of the curse lifting/breaking virtues of iron.

Traditional magic, being quite pragmatic in nature, has never shied away from new advances; as long as they are useful and an enhancement to efficacy. Thus with the advent of photography, once it became widely accessible to the populace, a new weapon was added to the arsenal of image magic, which again it must be remembered has always been employed for both good or for ill. If a photograph of the black witch can be obtained, the victim of maleficia might lift the evil influence from their home by writing the evil-doer's name across their image at the hearth before casting it into a good fire.

In West Country tradition, a number of devices may be made, and rites performed against the black witch, employing pins, nails, and thorns. The victim of maleficia might have a bottle and gather together many pins. Whilst muttering of the ways in which the black witch is to suffer, the pins are to be dropped into the bottle until it is full. This device, must be buried, or installed in some secret place, preferably in the vicinity of the black witch herself, and there left. As the spinous mass of pins rust, so shall the black witch fail in strength and health and become devoid of power.

Both the garlic and the onion have a long tradition of employment to provide protection against evil influences and powers. To inflict great pains and suffering upon the black witch; forcing her to lift her influence and rendering her magically impotent thereafter, an onion will be stuck full with many pins. Throughout their inserting, mutterings shall be made over the device of the black witch's fate. The profusely pin-stuck onion, run through, or affixed with black tatters or cord, is then to be hung in some out of the way place within the home, and there left to work its 'turning' influence.

Prepared in like manner, an onion may be stuck with many iron nails. This device is to be taken to a place where the black witch is known to walk regularly. Here it is to be secreted and left; each time the witch passes by the device she shall be weakened and she will be rendered powerless.

The heart, a seat of power, is likewise to be found pierced and transfixed within traditional 'turning' magic. The one bewitched may work a rite of counter-blasting employing an animal heart. The heart is to be stuck all over with as many pins as can be gathered, and a fire built. The pin-stuck heart is then to be secured above the fire to roast and be watched over as suffering and wasting is inflicted upon the black witch. Such torment can be inflicted in a similar but slower manner by hanging the pin-stuck heart within the chimney above the hearth-fire. As the heart is installed, the one bewitched will say;

"May Each Pin
Thus stuck in
This poor heart
In hers go
Who hurts me so
Till she departs"

Where an animal has died as a result of the evil influence of the black witch, its heart is to be removed by its owner to be employed in like manner for sticking and 'turning' magic. This heart is to be stuck all over with pins and whitethorns, and hung up within the chimney. With its withering above the hearth-fire, the heart, health, and power of the black witch shall wither also.

In many cases of traditional West Country 'turning' magic, the object of the suffering inflicted upon the black witch, is to force her to come to her victim to confess. Here the evil-doer will lift the ill-influence, begging for the torment to be stopped, with the additional benefit of the black witch's identity being revealed. One such method requires the one bewitched to cut a square of turf, which is to be pierced profusely with as many pins as can be gathered. A fire is then to be built and lit upon this, causing such torment to the black witch that they shall be forced to come to their victim, to confess and to lift her maleficia.

To destroy the black witch's power, 'fixing' or 'pinning down' magic may be employed with the use of iron nails, and maiden nails procured from the blacksmith are especially and famously prized for such work. When the identity of the black witch is known, the nails are to be taken by stealth to her abode and struck deep into the threshold of her door. The powers of the black witch will thereafter be drained from her upon crossing her threshold.

Another 'pinning down' method for the same purpose employs footstep magic. The one bewitched is to observe the black witch walking, where a discernable footprint has been left, the one bewitched must approach it and by stealth drive a maiden nail deep into the footprint's centre. Thus shall the ill-influence be lifted, and thereafter the black witch shall suffer great pain and will be devoid of power for as long as the nail remains undiscovered and in place.

Weather Witchcraft
✠

The arts of influencing the weather (be they brought into use for benevolent purposes, such as conjuring rains to quench parched lands, blessing events with glorious sunshine and providing sailors with a good wind; or for the malevolent conjurations of rain, wind and storm for disruption, punishment and calamity), fall within the darker and mysterious ways of the witch's craft and spirit-work.

To conjure rains, for good or for ill, the witch may 'Rake Down the Rain'. This is done by dragging a rake, with its down-side turned to point upward toward the skies. The witch might perform such an act within the circle of Arte, muttering conjurations of the kind of rain desired, where, when and for how long it is to fall, as the circumambulations are made, possibly around a smoking vessel of burning ferns.

For the black work of storm conjuration; causing lashing rains, tempests and thunder to come rolling in across sea and land, the witch may prepare a vessel of water within their circle of Arte. With spirits of the work raised, the witch shall crouch low and there, over the encompassed vessel, blow with much might, howling, shrieking and terrible incantations of the storm.

In work where it is desired that a certain ship be sunk or wrecked, it is a sign of the success of the operation if the vessel of water should be overturned during the great exertion of dark will, witch-power, and spirit-force.

The practitioner who has proper knowledge of the squares may summon forth storms by the aid of these signs and their spirits. With the sign before them, they shall, with raised staff, make their conjurations for the desired storm; touching then the sign upon its upper face. To cause such storms to cease, then shall they raise their staff in banishment and touch then the sign upon its under side:

For Rain

For Thunder

Circles of Power
✠

The circle, in form, in motion, and in gesture, is inextricably linked in the popular mind to the activities of witchcraft and the practices of magic from the lowest to the highest in kind. The functions performed by the circles of the witch, in both their low and higher workings, do however differ in nature from those employed within the workings of the high ceremonial magician who, predominantly it seems, seeks the virtues of protection and containment from such devices for the successful execution of their arte.

The diversity of ways in which the circle is employed within the West Country witch's art, it could be said, are all drawn to enable the witch to exert their total will over the object of the working encompassed. From the completed circle there is no exit for escape, and no entrance for the interference or pollution from external influences; thus for the object so ensorcelled, the interior of the encompassment becomes the totality of their environment, from which all possibilities outside those of the total will of the witch have been cut off into non-existence and impossibility, and the object is transfixed in the witch's eye.

These characteristics of the circle, as employed by witches and folk-magical practitioners, can be clearly seen within the old art of adder charming. Here, we find the ashen staff employed to mark out the ring (whether visible or not), circumscribing the serpent. Within the circumference of this demarcation, the creature is instantly captive and unable to cross the encompassing boundary.

We may see the same intent in operation within the employment of the circle for the purposes of cure-magic and 'blessing'. Whether the patient, animal or human, or place to be blessed is circumambulated entirely by the witch as the work is done, or the ailment itself is circled by finger, gesture of hand, application of substance, or by staff, the witch again seeks to exert their total will and influence over the object of their work. Within curative practices, the direction of the circle's forming is of some importance, for those made in the direction 'against the sun' are, in general, employed for the purposes of diminishment, removal and ending, whilst within those made in the direction 'with the sun' will the curative, regenerative influences and virtues be imparted. So, be it burn, bite, wart, ring-worm or any other physical grievance, the witch may bring death upon the ailment and birth forth regeneration and a return to health.

Conversely, West Country circle magic encompasses also malefic acts of vengeance, blasting and the bringing about of illness and death. Within the 'killing circle', the witch lays the fatal influence, and the circle drawn is the life-circle of their victim; drawn from its beginning to its ending and brought into completion. Thus for the object of the working there is no future left in life. The 'killing circle', drawn about a representation of the victim; such as a candle – named and then extinguished at the circle's closure, or their likeness, is formed with the intent of bringing about sudden illness and death, or even instant death. The witch might even, by stealth, pace the killing circle; marking it by staff or audaciously into visual manifestation by chalk, around their victim in actuality to impart upon them the same fate.

The more incautious might make the killing circle upon a path walked by their intended victim, when in surety that they will be the very next to walk it. As soon as the victim steps into the circle left for them, the fatal influence is immediately imparted upon them resulting in instant death in some cases, sudden illness leading to death in others.

It doesn't take the most perspicacious to see that this is far from the most circumspect method of operating, for as tradition warns; one can never be entirely certain of who will be the very next to walk any given path, and there is every risk that the influence will be imparted upon someone for whom it was entirely unintended.

With this method there is also the caveat that, if the intended victim becomes by whatever means aware of the witch's connivance against them, they are then empowered to neutralise the killing circle by throwing some poor animal, usually a chicken, into it to receive the fatal influence thus rendering the malignly circumscribed area safe to pass through.

Thus we can see why the witch might seek to operate less precariously to direct 'blastings' by means of 'magical links' such as candles representative of the victim, prepared likenesses, photographs, clothing or other intimate belongings of the intended victim etc. With the aid of such things, the circle for the purposes of killing or cursing can be employed with no less efficacy than one drawn for the victim to step into in actual physicality.

In West Country tradition, such circles are usually worked upon the hearth. Often the ashes of the hearth fire are employed to form the circle within which to lay the curse. Gunpowder has also been used in this way, usually for the purposes of causing fever and illness, with a small trail leading to the circle within which the prepared magical link will be placed. Over it are the words and incantations of the curse muttered, and at their climax the powder trail and circle are ignited with a dramatic, loud and smoky flash encircling the ensorcelled victim; a visually potent and impacting method for 'blasting'.

In League with the Devil
✠

Interactions with spirit entities, traditionally enjoyed in Cornwall and the West Country by ordinary folk and witches alike; such as the leaving of a penny on the table as a payment for the Piskies who will take it in exchange for cleaning the house, or leaving water offerings to them before the hearth-stone are widely known. However, there are far deeper and seemingly darker relationships of a numinous nature traditionally enjoyed by the West Country witch.

As we have clearly seen, the 'true breed' of Cornish and West Country witch is a practitioner of 'double-ways', and by long standing tradition these twin powers to bless and to blast are derived from the 'Old One' of many names; Bucca Dhu, 'Old Nick', and The Devil being but three.

Even amongst the 'white' practitioners, consulted by the ordinary folk for their wisdom and magical aid for all manner of requirements, there have always been those regarded, or suspected, as being witches of a 'deeper dye'; those whose Craft is empowered by their mysterious dealings, compacts, and regular conferences with The Devil.

The methods via which the traditional Cornish and West Country witch might make such compacts and enter consciously into the 'Old Craft', vary from the outwardly simple and chthonic, to rites of a seemingly blasphemous nature; yet concealing mysteries of the divine light, gnosis and apotheosis.

Well known via the popular witch-lore of Cornwall are the stories surrounding the various remote Logan Stones, or 'Logging Stones'. Here the folkloric collectors suggest various initiatory witch-rites in which the aspirant ventures out to such a stone, and there, under the cover of midnight and at the full of the moon, one of a variety of simple rites is to be observed. In all cases that familiar and lunar magical number nine is a central feature; whether the aspirant is to circumambulate nine times around the stone against the sun, to touch the stone nine times, or to make nine attempts to climb upon and off the stone without causing it to rock.

To such seemingly simple rites of folklore, the nearest comparable rites and practices actually observed by witches of the old persuasion in Cornwall involve dedications, sacrifices and loci-specific rites performed under the direction of an initiated witch, wise-woman or cunning-man. Such activities are always of a highly challenging nature and not for the faint-hearted, and, as I can confirm, to make one's way at the dead of night to a 'Logging Stone' is certainly not without its difficulties. Yet, at such a striven for site, here is the 'Old One' called upon with alarming potency and the witch's initiation imparted deep into the bones via the chthonic pulse.

In old West Country belief, the gifts imparted via the witch's diabolic compact with the Bucca Dhu; the Black God or Devil, include the ability to send forth one's will or 'spirit' in bestial form, or else via the received familiar spirit, to carry out the double-ways work of the witch and convey her magical influence upon man or beast.

Of all the many theriomorphous entities of traditional witch-lore, the most inextricable and symbiotic relationship is to be found between the West Country witch and the toad.

The toad is synonymous with, and emblematic of, both the Devil and the witch in old West Country lore. Sometimes the Devil would appear to the witch in the form of a toad, and, as an act of ritual homage to the one from whom they derive their powers, the witch would kiss the toad upon its mouth. The toad it seems was both the spirit familiar of choice, and the preferred form for travelling forth in spirit amongst West Country witches.

Drawing distinction between the witch, her own spirit sent forth in toad form, and her batrachian spirit familiar, is a great difficulty, if not an impossibility; as is evidenced in the folklore of families and individuals who have, in whatever way, aroused the witch's anger only to find themselves terrorised by a sudden visitation from

128

a mysterious great toad. Often, as is sadly the case with people of great ignorance, the poor creature is put to a brutal death. Sometimes this takes a number of attempts; the toad 'regenerating' each time before finally succumbing to death, or disappearing from the scene. Later the witch is discovered, sometimes dead, with injuries corresponding to those previously inflicted upon the toad. For those who have offended the witch however, the matter is not done with; for the witch has by the visitation already imparted her influence, and dire misfortunes always follow.

As is the case with the initiatory rites of the 'Logging Stones', the folklorist will be familiar also with the 'Churchyard and Toad-Breath' rite of diabolic witch-initiation. Within this rite, we are told by collectors such as the Reverend R.S. Hawker, that the aspirant witch must go to chancel to partake of the sacrament, yet hiding away the bread when accepted from the priest. The aspirant shall then return with the bread to the churchyard, and go to the northern side and there begin three circumambulations around the church, backwards and in the direction against the sun, repeating all the while backwards the Lord's Prayer. Upon returning to the north for the third time, there shall the aspirant be met with a great toad to whom the aspirant is to feed the bread. Then shall the toad breath thrice upon the aspirant; who thereafter shall be a strong witch, having by this act conferred upon him/her all the powers of the Arte.

Again, to such curiosities of folklore, there are comparable rites of concealed mystery observed by some within the Cornish and West Country Old Craft. Knowledge of such rites, as is proper, is imparted from one initiate to another, yet their mysteries may be pondered by exploration of the relationship betwixt the West Country witch and the toad.

There is a marked difference between the true West Country 'toad witch' and those 'toad doctors' of folk-magical tradition who would wrest and cut from the living creatures various body parts for use in their curative charms. To the profane and ignorant, the toad is often regarded as being only a hideous vessel for all things loathsome, repugnant, abhorrent, and ultimately of evil. Thus have such people reacted with fear at catching sight of a toad which sadly, and all too often, would result in the poor creature being put without hesitation to some truculent and overly heavy-handed death. A toad appearing on the doorstep would often be taken as a sign that the household was under the influence of a witch's curse, whilst more anciently in other cultures such a thing would instead be taken as a blessed sign of good fortune and prosperity. Those of intelligence would be more inclined to share the latter view, for as wise old folk know; the toad is a good thing to have in the garden and those of the Old Craft have been known to keep gardens well stocked with toads; for with their presence is brought blessing and abundance.

The ways and approach of the West Country toad witch differ also from their colleagues of East Anglia and other areas, whose initiatory mystery cult would appear to be entered into almost entirely by masculine companie. It is thus perhaps comprehensible why their rites involve the disassembly of the toad; reducing its form to one part, rather like the systematic stripping down of a mechanism in search of a particular vital component piece. Such rites have often involved the killing of the toad in particularly cold-hearted ways, although it is known that some initiates have employed already dead toads gifted to them by chance. By contrast, the cult of the West Country toad witch embraces the toad in whole, unmolested form, in order to achieve the same ends. Whilst its initiates are numbered by both women and men, this is very much a feminine cult in nature and approach; in which the toad is cosseted and adored with a motherly passion. To such a witch, the toad with its delicate, soft, round, yet deathly cold form, and with its little arms and legs, tiny fingers and toes, is beheld as a beautiful otherworldly baby whom the witch will gladly nourish with blood drawn forth from her veins or milk from her breast. Certainly, many witches of Cornwall, Devon and the West Country have had wisdom of the gifts, as well as the costs, brought by the special maintaining and preserving of a relationship, or union, with toad spirits.

It is little wonder that such a relationship should exist, and that witch and toad are so intimately bound in ancient affinity, for the toad, like the witch, is a creature of liminality. Being born forth from the waters of the underworld to walk upon the land, to enter into the earth and maintain a state of death-like stillness through the harshness of winter, to emerge reborn from the tomb, returning to the waters to breed; in the toad we clearly have a creature of passage between the worlds, between life, death, and resurrection and a vehicle of the chthonic and aqueous forces. The toad is also, of course, a creature of transformation; the visually transformative nature of toads, frogs and newts in their metamorphosis from the egg to adult is inherently magical to behold. Being a creature of liminality and of passage between the worlds, it is quite understandable why, to the witch, the toad should be regarded also as a vehicle for the wisdom of the dead and of the Faery Folk. In the toxicity of the toad's 'venoms' we may find ancient associations with magical influence, defence, vision and spirit-flight.

It is the mutual affinity between witch and toad, and the old ways of sympathetic magic employed by the witch and the ordinary folk alike, which will undoubtedly have been behind the past employment of the toad by ordinary folk against witchery. In Devonshire, folk would hang a bag of patterned fabric containing a toad within their cottages as a protective charm to keep witches away. The old belief once also held by Devonians that toads should be caught and put to death by burning as witches, affirm the traditional knowledge that there is no separation between witch and toad.

The Black Toad of Cornish and West Country Old Craft is, in many ways, akin to the 'Black Toad' of English alchemical tradition. Here we find an emblematic vessel-avatar of the 'earth of the philosophers', the 'First Matter' and the very root and beginning of 'The Work'. Within the arcanum of the alchemical Black Toad we find also an emblem of the power of attraction, sexual force, the attraction of the opposites where 'All is One', thus is the Black Toad emblematic of the beginning and the end of the work.

The creature of the toad, beheld by some to be *"ugly and venomous, wears yet a precious jewel in his head."* Belief in such an occult jewel as the 'toad-stone', 'Borax' or 'Stelon' may in some ways be a relation of the traditions surrounding the prized toad-bone.

Held by the ignorant to be a loathed and feared creature of poison, darkness, death, and entirely evil in nature, yet the more enlightened behold a creature of good fortune, healing, fertility and love. To the wise, that which appears to others 'dark' and 'evil' contains the 'Occultum Lapidem'. The West Country toad-witches know this to be true of the toad, and have their own guarded understanding of this mystery. From the dark comes forth the divine light of wisdom as the witch is the mother of the powers she bears forth. The West Country Toad witch in her motherly cosseting of the toad is the mother of light from the dark; wondrously blessed and accursed in union; feeding her toad of her body's life blood; the very vehicle of her power.

Bibliography

An Joan The Crone; The History and Craft of the Cornish Witch, Kelvin Jones, Oakmagic Publications

Cornish Charms and Witchcraft, Anonymous, Tor Mark Press

Cornish Feasts and Folklore, M.A Courtney, Beare and Son

Cornish Superstitions, Kelvin Jones, Oakmagic Publications

Customs and Superstitions of East Cornwall, Jonathan and Thomas Couch, Oakmagic Publications

Devon Witchcraft and Folk Ways, Sarah Hewett, Troy Books

Folklore and Witchcraft of Devon and Cornwall, Ed. Kelvin Jones, Oakmagic Publications

Occult Cornwall, Kelvin Jones, Oakmagic Publications

Popular Magic - Cunning-folk in English History, Owen Davies, Hambledon Continuum

Bibliography

The Book of the Sacred Magic of Abramelin the Mage, S.L. MacGregor Mathers, 1900 (translated from 15th century French mauscript), various publishers

The Cornish Witch-Finder, William Henry Paynter, Ed. Jason Semmens, The federation of Old Cornwall Societies

The Customs, Superstitions and Legends of the County of Somerset, Charles Henry Poole, various publishers

The Discoverie of Witchcraft, Reginald Scot, 1584, various publishers

The Living Stones, Ithell Colquhoun, Peter Owen

The Magus, Francis Barrett, 1801, various publishers

The Witchcraft and Folklore of Dartmoor, Ruth E.St. Leger-Gordon, Robert Hale

Traditional Witchcraft - A Cornish Book of Ways, Gemma Gary, Troy Books

West Country Folklore, Roy and Ursula Radford, Peninsular press

West Country Witchcraft, Roy and Ursula Radford, Peninsular Press

West Country Witches, Michael Howard, Three Hands Press

White Witches - A Study of Charmers, Rose Mullins, PR Publishing

Witchcraft in Cornwall, Kelvin Jones, Oakmagic Publications

Index

136